Understanding the
War in Afghanistan

Understanding the War in Afghanistan

A Guide to the Land, the People, and the Conflict

by Joseph J. Collins

Skyhorse Publishing

All inquiries should be addressed to Skyhorse Publishing, 307 West 36th Street, 11th Floor, New York, NY 10018.

Skyhorse Publishing books may be purchased in bulk at special discounts for sales promotion, corporate gifts, fund-raising, or educational purposes. Special editions can also be created to specifications. For details, contact the Special Sales Department, Skyhorse Publishing, 307 West 36th Street, 11th Floor, New York, NY 10018 or info@skyhorsepublishing.com.

Skyhorse® and Skyhorse Publishing® are registered trademarks of Skyhorse Publishing, Inc.®, a Delaware corporation.

Visit our website at www.skyhorsepublishing.com.

10 9 8 7 6 5 4 3 2 1

Library of Congress Cataloging-in-Publication Data is available on file.
ISBN: 978-1-62087-482-0

Printed in the United States of America

Contents

Chapters

Opening Thoughts

As we confront [future] decisions, it is well to remember what is at stake. If we fail in Afghanistan, the state will fragment; there is no power center yet standing on its feet and capable of taking our place. If Afghanistan fragments, then parts of the country will again become the natural base for those who have attacked not only us but also London and Madrid and who have planned to blow up planes over the Atlantic. And a fragmented Afghanistan will become the strategic rear and base for extremism in Pakistan, a nation of 155 million people that is armed with nuclear weapons. This will allow and facilitate support for extremist movements across the huge swath of energy-rich Central Asia, as was the case in the 1990s.

—Ambassador Ronald E. Neumann, *The Other War: Winning and Losing in Afghanistan*[1]

Similarly, a setback in Afghanistan would be enormously empowering to jihadists everywhere in the world but would also inflict enormous reputational damage on the United States (as the perception of U.S. failure in Iraq in 2003–2006 did). Failure after the President recommitted the United States to succeed in Afghanistan would support the notion that America is incapable of capitalizing on its military power and advantages (including the development of an extremely capable force for conducting counterinsurgency operations). It would make dealing with potential problems in Pakistan, Yemen, and Somalia (to name a few) enormously harder.

—Ambassador Eric Edelman, *Understanding America's Contested Primacy*[2]

Preface

This monograph is an intellectual primer on war in Afghanistan. I come to this task through a string of accidents that has kept me involved with war in Afghanistan as a Soldier and an academic for over 30 years. It began in graduate school at Columbia University in New York City, where I was privileged to study with some of the Nation's greatest experts on the Soviet Union and Central Europe, and with another superb crew of scholars on war and peace issues. These interests came together with the Soviet invasion of Afghanistan.

From 1980 to 1984, I worked on my dissertation on the Soviet invasion under the guidance of two consummate professionals: Professors Marshall Shulman, the former Advisor to Secretary of State Cyrus Vance on Soviet affairs; and Zalmay Khalilzad, a young academic strategist who later became a colleague in the Pentagon and still later Ambassador to Afghanistan, his boyhood home, and then to Iraq. Three colleagues at West Point were very helpful in my study of Afghanistan: then-Colonel Ty Cobb, my boss, and a future senior director on the National Security Council (NSC) staff; Visiting Professor Jerry Hudson, a superb Soviet expert and a demanding coach; and the late Louis Dupree, the world's leading Afghanistan specialist, a scholar with a soldier's heart. David Isby and Bill Olson have also been friends and tutors on Southwest Asia since 1980. My former student and Army colleague Tom Lynch has joined their ranks and has been especially helpful on the issue of modern-day Pakistan.

Sadly, a few years after leaving Columbia and my concurrent teaching tour in the Department of Social Sciences at West Point, I watched the Afghan war with the Soviet Union end, only to be replaced by a civil war, then a war against the Taliban, and then a war prosecuted by the Taliban and al Qaeda against the Northern Alliance. As a result of this endless war, Afghanistan has become one of the most devastated countries on Earth.

In 2001, as Deputy Assistant Secretary of Defense for Stability Operations (2001–2004), I was privileged to lead a team of Pentagon policy experts who worked a key part of the Pentagon's Afghanistan portfolio. Inside the Pentagon, we took our orders from Under Secretary Doug Feith and worked closely with his deputy, Bill Luti, and later the Defense Department's senior reconstruction and stabilization coordinator Dov Zakheim, the department's comptroller. My team interacted with an active and productive interagency effort led by Ambassador Bill Taylor, and later the NSC staff's Tony Harriman. In my seven trips to the region, the devastation of the country and the difficulty of counterinsurgency stood out starkly. On my last trip, I flew home next to the gurney of a severely wounded paratrooper from the Alaska-based 4th Brigade Combat Team (Airborne) of 25th Infantry Division. The severity of his wounds and the devotion of his Air Force medics were vivid reminders of the costs of this war and the continuing sacrifice of our men and women in uniform.

I returned to academic life in 2004 and now teach at the National War College, where I have been engaged in a full-time study of war on the low end of the conflict spectrum. Teaching remains the ultimate learning experience, and this monograph owes much to the intellectual stimulation my students provide. It could not have come about without the help of many people. I would like to thank Vice Admiral Ann Rondeau, USN, President of the National Defense University, and Major General Robert Steel, USAF, then-Commandant of the National War College, for allowing me a sabbatical to complete this and other projects. My colleagues, Dan Caldwell of Pepperdine University; Jacqueline

Hazelton of Harvard University's Belfer Center; Daniel Weggeland, a veteran of service in Afghanistan on the development and counterinsurgency fronts; Colonel Vince Dreyer, USA, an Afghanistan veteran turned academic expert; former Ambassador Ron Neumann; Jeff Hayes of the NSC staff; and Lieutenant Colonel Jason Boehm, USMC, of the Joint Staff, and Liz Packard of U.S. Central Command read the manuscript and made great suggestions. Special thanks go to Admiral James Stavridis, Supreme Allied Commander Europe. He, Colonel Mike Howard, USA, and others at Supreme Headquarters Allied Powers Europe made many insightful comments on the manuscript. General Peter Chiarelli, the Vice Chief of Staff of the Army, and Lieutenant General Chuck Jacoby, the Joint Staff, J5, were supportive throughout. As always, the creative team at NDU Press added immeasurably to the final product.

My wife Anita, along with my sons Joseph and Jude and their families, are my life and my moral support. They join me in dedicating this monograph to the military personnel, diplomats, and civil servants who have served in Iraq and Afghanistan. To paraphrase Sir Winston Churchill, as we approach the 10th anniversary of 9/11, never have so many Americans owed so much to so few of their countrymen. As always, despite all of this support and assistance, any mistakes in this monograph are my own.

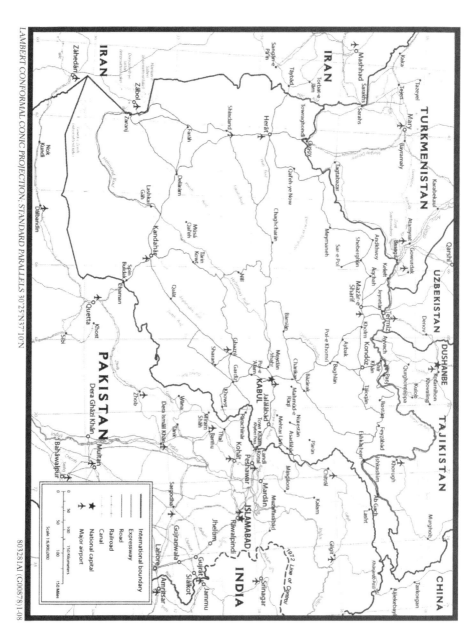

Note: For high-resolution, full-color maps, please visit www.skyhorsepublishing.com.

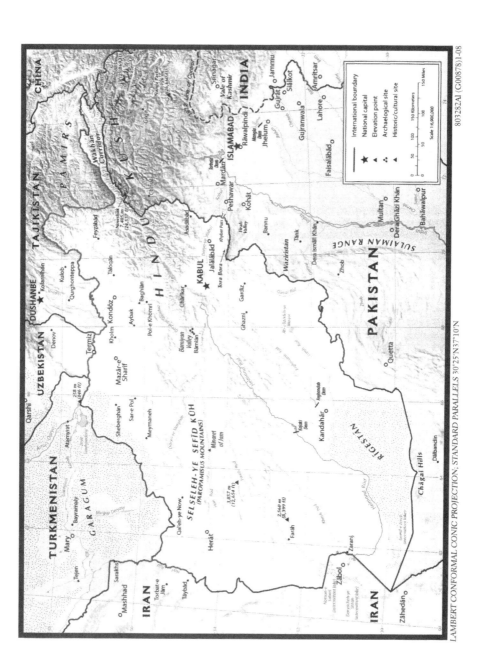

Physiography

Administrative Divisions

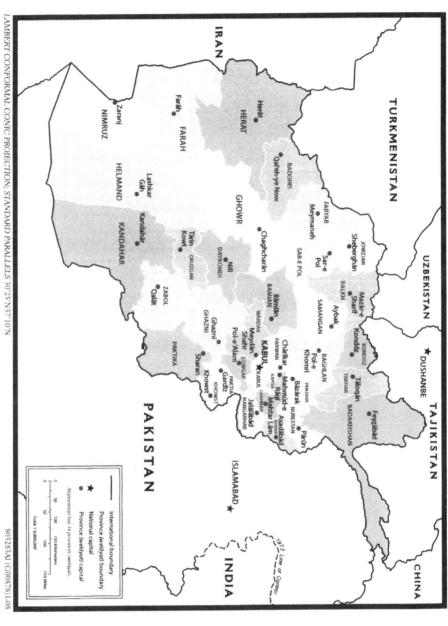

LAMBERT CONFORMAL CONIC PROJECTION; STANDARD PARALLELS 30°25'N 37°10'N

803283AI (C00878)1-08

IRAN

TURKMENISTAN

UZBEKISTAN

★ DUSHANBE

TAJIKISTAN

CHINA

PAKISTAN

ISLAMABAD ★

INDIA

1972 Line of Control

NIMRUZ

Zaranj

Farāh

FARAH

Herāt

HERAT

Qaleh-ye Now

BADGHIS

HELMAND

GHOWR

Lashkar
Gāh

Kandahār

KANDAHAR

Chaghcharān

Tarīn
Kowt

DAYKONDI

URUZGAN

Nīlī

Qalāt

ZABOL

Meymaneh

FARYAB

Sar-e
Pol

SAR-E POL

Sheberghān

JOWZJAN

Mazār-e
Sharīf

BALKH

Aybak

SAMANGAN

Bāmīān

BAMIAN

WARDAK

Meydān
Shahr

Pol-e Alam

LOWGAR

KABUL
★ KABUL

PARWAN

Chārīkar

KAPISA

Mahmūd-e
Asadābād

Pol-e
Khomrī

BAGHLAN

Bāzārak

PANJSHIR

NURISTAN

Pārūn

Kondoz

KONDOZ

TAKHAR

Tāloqān

Feyzābād

BADAKHSHAN

Ghaznī

GHAZNI

KHOWST

Gardīz

PAKTIA

Sharan

PAKTIKA

Khowst

Rāgī

NANGARHAR

Jalālābād

Mehtar Lām

LAGHMAN

KONAR

Ethnolinguistic Groups

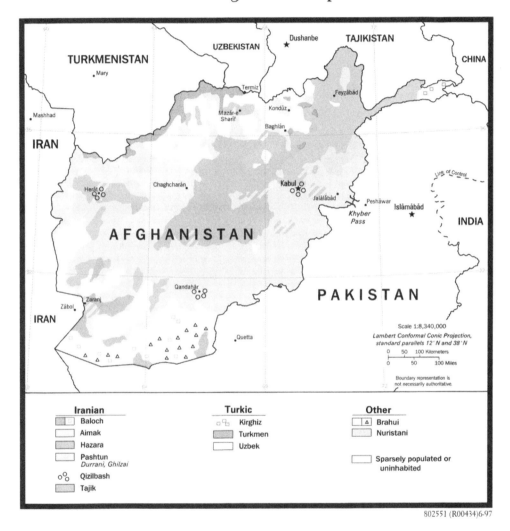

802551 (R00434)6-97

Introduction

This monograph aims to provide military leaders, civil servants, diplomats, and students with the intellectual basis they need to prepare for further study or for assignments in Afghanistan, a nation that has been at war for 33 years. Officers in the Af-Pak Hands Program may also find it a useful starting point, but their intensive studies will quickly take them beyond the scope of this work. Students or scholars may also find it a useful primer for learning about Afghanistan. By analyzing the land and its people, recapping Afghan history, and assessing the current situation, this work hopes to set a foundation upon which leaders and scholars can begin their preparation for more specific tasks. It also will examine the range of choice for future U.S. policy toward Afghanistan and give suggestions for future study.

Much of the outline of recent events will be familiar to many readers. Just 2 days before their 9/11 attack on the United States, al Qaeda operatives posing as journalists succeeded in assassinating the commander of Northern Alliance forces, Ahmed Shah Massoud, inside his own headquarters in northern Afghanistan. This act was an al Qaeda favor to its Taliban brothers, a reward for their past support, and a down payment on the grief that was about to descend on the Taliban from the United States and its allies. With the heinous terrorist acts of 9/9 and 9/11, the Afghan and American people became tied together in a common war against al Qaeda and its fellow traveler, the Taliban.

After al Qaeda bombed our Embassies in Kenya and Tanzania in 1998, the United States, the Kingdom of Saudi Arabia, and others asked the Taliban to surrender Osama bin Laden. They refused. After al Qaeda's attacks on New York, the Pentagon, and in Pennsylvania, the Taliban again refused to turn over Osama bin Laden and his accomplices. With the backing of its allies and a United Nations (UN) Security Council Resolution, the United States took decisive action. With Special Operations Forces (SOF), CIA operatives, and U.S. airpower in support, the Northern Alliance and friendly Pashtun tribes in the south were able to vanquish the Taliban forces and chase them and their al Qaeda allies into Iran and Pakistan. Sadly, both Mullah Omar and Osama bin Laden escaped along with many of their key subordinates. An international conference established an interim government with Northern Alliance and anti-Taliban Pashtun representatives. Hamid Karzai was named its interim leader.

The initial phases of Operation *Enduring Freedom* (OEF) in Afghanistan were successful but not decisive. From 2002 to 2005, a small American and international force tried to help Afghanistan to its feet. There was modest and mainly unopposed progress in development, governance, and the rule of law. With a "small footprint" force and not very much aid money, efforts by the Kabul government and its partners were not enough. The Taliban plotted a comeback and made detailed preparations from its sanctuary in Pakistan. With a priority on operations in Iraq, the United States was surprised at the virulence of the Taliban attack that began in earnest in 2005. India attempted to offset Pakistani influence through aid and economic policy. Iran tried hard to protect its interests in the west, and erratically aided the Taliban—its former enemy—in order to block the United States. China and Russia looked on warily, often seeking economic benefits. The Kingdom of Saudi Arabia later tried to help make peace but was frustrated by the links between the Taliban and the Kingdom's mortal enemy, al Qaeda.

Only in 2008, however, after the war in Iraq began to subside, was the United States able to focus on its serious predicament in Afghanistan. The Obama administration redoubled U.S. efforts, stepped up drone attacks against insurgent and terrorist leaders, and surged U.S. civilian and military assets in hopes of bringing about conditions conducive to peace. At the same time, President Barack Obama declared that he would not support an endless war in Afghanistan. He noted his intention to begin a conditions-based withdrawal of American forces in the summer of 2011. Later, the NATO nations at the Lisbon Summit established a target date of 2014 for Afghanistan to take charge of its security nationwide.

How did the United States and its allies get to where they are today? How can that coalition understand the many wars in Afghanistan over the past 33 years? How should it define its interests today? How can this group of nearly 50 nations—working together as the International Security Assistance Force (ISAF)—help to bring this war to an end? To answer these questions, it is important to first examine the land, its people, and their culture (chapter 1). Next, we have to grapple with Afghan history (chapter 2), the Soviet-Afghan War (chapter 3), and the conflicts that followed it (chapters 4 and 5). As we move to the current conflict, we must also understand the basic theory and concepts that underpin counterinsurgency in the 21st century (chapter 6). This enables us to comprehend what happened during the 2002–2010 timeframe (chapters 7 and 8). Finally, we have to examine the potential choices that national leaders face for the future (chapter 9). Throughout the text, I draw heavily on my own published work with minimal citations.[1] The data in this study are the best available in January 2011.

1. Land, People, and Culture

Geography, demography, and culture are among the great "givens" of life. They can influence every aspect of our existence. Knowing about them is the first step in learning about a state, its peoples, and its policies.

Afghanistan is slightly smaller than Texas, roughly 647,500 square kilometers. Looking at the map, its most dominant feature is the Hindu Kush mountains, which rise to 7,485 meters and cover all but the north central and southwest portions of the country.[1] Even Kabul, the capital, lies at 1,789 meters in elevation. Semi-desert terrain is common in the south and west and in the flatter areas. Snow melt and a handful of rivers, aided by intricate and sometimes ancient irrigation systems, bring water to farmland in many regions. Only 14 percent of the land is arable, a great limitation since farming and herding are the most common occupations. Afghanistan has as much as $1 trillion to $3 trillion in mineral wealth, much of which was recently rediscovered and not yet exploited.[2]

Politically, Afghanistan today has an external border with Pakistan measuring 2,430 kilometers (km), disputed since it was drawn by the British along the Durand Line in 1893. It also has a border in the west with Iran measuring 936 km as well as significant borders with the former Soviet republics and now independent nations of Turkmenistan (744 km), Uzbekistan (137 km), and Tajikistan (1,206 km). There is also a short border with China (76 km) in the mountainous, sparsely populated Wakhan Corridor in the northeast. Internally, Afghanistan is divided into 34 provinces, which are subdivided into nearly 400 districts. Afghanistan has a poor nationwide transportation network. A primary road, often referred to as the Ring Road, connects the major cities: Kabul in the east, Kandahar in the south, Herat in the west, and Mazar-i-Sharif in the north. It was built with U.S. and Soviet help in the 1960s and rebuilt by the United States, its coalition partners, and international financial institutions (IFIs) after 2001. Other primary roads connect Kabul to Jalalabad in the east, not far from the Pakistan border. Another major road runs from Kandahar in the south to the Chaman crossing, and then into the Baluchistan Province of Pakistan. To compete with the Pakistani geographic advantage, India and Iran have also built new roads, one of which runs north from the Iranian port of Charbahar into the province of Nimruz in Afghanistan, ultimately linking up with the Ring Road in Delaram. Another Iranian-built road connects Islam Qala with Herat in western Afghanistan. Thousands of kilometers of secondary and tertiary roads have been built by allied forces, supporting aid agencies, and IFIs. American generals and diplomats generally agree with the pithy observation of the current Ambassador and former commanding general, Karl Eikenberry: "Where the roads end, the Taliban begins."[3]

Air and rail assets present a contrast. Air travel is fairly well developed for such a poor country. There are major airports in Kabul, at the Bagram military facility north of Kabul, and in Kandahar. Mazar-i-Sharif is the logistic hub to the north, and Jalalabad in the east, and Herat and Shindand in the far west, also have airports. There are only 75 km of railroad, connecting the north to Uzbekistan.

The population of Afghanistan is uncertain, but most experts believe it to be in the range of 28–30 million people. Despite substantial repatriation, more than two million Afghans remain refugees in Iran and Pakistan. The population is young, with 44.6 percent under the age of 15 years. The relatively high growth rate of 2.6 percent is moderated by some of the highest infant and child mortality rates in the world. Life expectancy is 44 years. Less than 25 percent of Afghans live in urban areas compared to 67 percent of Iraqis. By definition, reconstruction or construction in Afghanistan will be about rural areas, which are some of the least developed in the world. On the UN Human Development Index, which measures the health, education, and economic life of a nation, Afghanistan has been consistently ranked in the bottom 10 countries in the world.

Afghanistan is a multiethnic Muslim state. The most dominant group is the Pashtuns (also called Pathans, Pushtuns, or Pakhtoons), estimated at 40–42 percent of the population. There may be as many as 400 tribes and clans of Pashtuns, although the war, refugee life, and the Taliban have subverted the power of tribal and clan leaders. The Pashtuns tend to live in the eastern and southern parts of the country, but pockets of Pashtuns can be found in the north. While there are approximately 12 million Pashtuns in Afghanistan, there are twice as many in Pakistan, mainly in the eastern parts, in Khyber Pakhtunkhwa (the former Northwest Frontier Province), the Federally Administered Tribal Areas (FATA), Baluchistan, and around Karachi. The 2,400 km border between Pakistan and Afghanistan is often ignored by Pashtun tribes living near it. Inside Afghanistan, perhaps the greatest intra-Pashtun fault line is between southern or Durrani Pashtuns and the eastern or Ghilzai Pashtuns. Inside Pakistan, tensions between Islamabad and the semiautonomous tribes are constant. The Pashtun tribes in the FATA of Pakistan and elsewhere have formed their own insurgent groups in recent years, the most notable of which is the Tehrik-e-Taliban Pakistan.[4]

The other major Afghan groups are the Tajiks at 27–30 percent, the Hazara at 15 percent, and the Uzbek and Turkmen at 9–10 percent of the total population. The remaining 13 percent or so come from smaller minorities: Nuristani, Pashai, Aimaq, and others. Languages are also mixed, with about half speaking Dari (Afghan Persian, the lingua franca); 35 percent speaking Pashto (or Pushtu, the language of the Pashtun); and 11 percent—mostly Uzbek and Turkmen—speaking Turkic languages. There are 30 known minor languages also spoken in Afghanistan.

Three groups dominate the non-Pashtun segment of Afghans. Together, they constitute a majority of the population. The Dari-speaking Tajiks are the second largest group. They are nontribal and dominate the populations of Kabul, Mazar-i-Sharif, and Herat. Most nonurban Tajiks are spread across the northeastern part of the country including the famous Panjshir Valley. While most Tajiks are farmers, they have "historically been the bedrock of the merchant community, bureaucrats, and educated clergy" in Afghanistan.[5] Many analysts believed that the Tajik formations under the late Commander Ahmed Shah Massoud were the most effective fighters in the anti-Soviet war. They formed the core of the Northern Alliance that retook Kabul in the fall of 2001.

The Hazaras, the next largest group, live mainly in the central high plateau and in the north. Many of them have distinctive Mongol-like features. Because of their appearance and the fact that most Hazaras are Shia Muslims, they have often been treated badly by other Afghans, with the Taliban being the last to mistreat them. For most of the modern era, aside from the Taliban period of rule, the Sunni-Shia schism has not been as divisive a factor in Afghanistan as it has been in Iraq.

The Turkic-speaking Uzbeks and Turkmen make up 10 percent of the Afghan population. Many Uzbek and Turkmen families moved from their non-Afghan homelands in Central Asia in the 20th century when the Bolsheviks took over all of the republics of the then–Soviet Union. The Uzbeks and Turkmen are famous for carpets and karakul sheep. The Uzbeks are considered highly effective fighters on the ground or on horseback.

Most Afghans (not "Afghanis," which refers to the local currency and is considered by some Afghans as bad form if used to refer to people) are Sunni Muslims (80 percent), with the balance—mainly Hazaras—being Shia Muslims. Prior to the Soviet invasion of 1979, many observers saw Afghans as rather laid-back Muslims. Tribal ways that run counter to Islam may still hold sway in a few isolated areas. Pashtuns are defined by their tribes and their folkways. As noted, however, these tribal structures have been severely stressed by wars. Many who grew up in Pakistani refugee camps lost track of their tribal roots, leaving them much more open to the influence of religious figures, called mullahs, and other nontribal leaders. In all, the strict observance of Islam has grown across Afghanistan since the war with the Soviet Union.

Since the Pashtuns dominate the nation's leadership as well as that of the Taliban, it is important to delve deeper into their culture. Pashtun culture revolves around the Pashtunwali, their pre-Islamic code of honor. It emphasizes honor, hospitality, protection of women, and revenge. Louis Dupree, the late eminent Western specialist on Afghanistan, described the Pashtunwali this way:

> to avenge blood
> to fight to the death for a person who has taken refuge with me
>   no matter what his lineage
> to defend to the last any property entrusted to me
> to be hospitable and provide for the safety of guests
> to refrain from killing a woman, a Hindu, a minstrel, or a boy
>   not yet circumcised
> to pardon an offense on the intercession of a woman of the
>   offender's lineage, a Sayyid, or a Mullah

to punish all adulterers with death

to refrain from killing a man who has entered a mosque or a
    shrine of a holy man . . . also to spare the life of a man who
    begs for quarter in battle.[6]

Pashtun culture has helped to keep Afghanistan independent, but it has also helped to make it a fractious place, rife with internal violence within and between families and clans. Even conflict between cousins is a thread in all too many stories in this part of the world. Pashtuns, however, have a tradition of tribal assemblies, or *jirgas*, that help them to resolve problems and make group decisions. The term *shura*, an Arabic expression meaning consultation, is also used to denote smaller consultative groupings. On a few occasions, the entire Afghan nation has formed a grand assembly, a *loya jirga*, to approve a constitution or select a national leader.

Xenophobia is another aspect of Afghan culture. Throughout Afghanistan, suspicion of foreigners is strong. This no doubt stems from insularity and frequent invasions. Afghans are independence-minded. The Pashtun warning to the government and to foreigners says it all: don't touch our women, our treasure, or our land. Non-Pashtun Afghans—58 percent of the population—generally share this attitude and have their own set of hard feelings toward the dominant Pashtuns. Afghans of all stripes have a strong sense of personal and national honor.

The Pashtuns form the largest group of Afghans and account for nearly all of today's insurgents inside the country. The Taliban (literally "students") started as an organized group in 1994. Although led by Afghan Pashtuns, Pakistan has supported the movement from the outset. The Taliban's roots reach back to the war with the Soviets and to the refugee Islamic school *madrassa* (*madaris* in the plural form) found in

Pakistan and in the countryside of southern Afghanistan. Often funded by Muslim charities from the Gulf, these madaris were rudimentary religious schools, but they were among the few schools of any sort that were open to Afghans or Afghan refugees during the civil war. The mullahs also fed and often housed their pupils. In these schools, country mullahs taught their often illiterate students to memorize the Koran and the *hadith* — the sayings of the Prophet. The students also learned to revere the conduct of jihad as holy war and observe the pure practices of the original Islam.

Many students became religious zealots, dedicated, honest, and without much to lose. Their beliefs were anti-Western and antimaterialist and favored old-time Islam, thus closely paralleling what Salafists preached. Ahmed Rashid, a Pakistani scholar-journalist, saw the Taliban this way:

> *These boys were from a generation that had never seen their country at peace. . . . They had no memories of their tribes, their elders, their neighbors nor the complex ethnic mix of peoples that often made up their villages and their homeland. These boys were what the war had thrown up like the sea's surrender on the beach of history. They had no memories of the past, no plans for the future while the present was everything. They were literally the orphans of the war, the rootless and the restless, the jobless and the economically deprived with little self-knowledge. They admired war because it was the only occupation they could possibly adapt to. Their simple belief in a messianic, puritan Islam which had been drummed into them by simple village mullahs was the only prop they could hold on to and which gave their lives some meaning.*[7]

Part Pashtunwali, part radical Islam, and part the blowback of war, the Taliban would first rescue their country from lawlessness and then abuse it, alienating the population and opening Afghanistan to international ridicule. The Taliban, however, would survive an ouster and later create an insurgency to try to take back power.

In all, the effects of geography, demography, and culture will echo through the history of Afghanistan. First, the country is rugged, landlocked, and difficult to get around in. It is also hard to conduct trade or military operations in such terrain. The lack of good roads combines with high elevations to complicate commerce, logistics, and military operations. Local Afghans are accustomed to the terrain and can outmaneuver the untrained or heavily burdened foreigner. Limited urbanization puts harsh demands on those who seek to protect the population as well. Geographic conditions also complicate the supply of a major expeditionary force operating 7,000 miles from the continental United States. Supplies have to be flown in, or more often, arrive by sea in Karachi, southern Pakistan, and must be trucked the length or width of the country to find an entryway into Afghanistan. Alternatively, supplies can follow a more tortuous northern route through southern Russia and Central Asia into northern Afghanistan. Another route begins in southeast Iran, but that, of course, is not available to the United States.

Second, Afghanistan is not rich in farmland or other natural resources. A low-level of factor endowments makes poverty a natural condition. Iran and Pakistan control the outlets to the sea and to major markets. Afghanistan has great potential mineral wealth, but it has been whispered about for decades and will require enormous investment and many years to exploit fully. Moreover, many developing countries have had great difficulties managing the foreign extraction of oil or minerals and subsequently absorbing and disbursing the profits.

Third, geography favors local and tribal power structures. While officials in Kabul have usually favored centralized arrangements, local officials or tribal leaders have always held much residual power over their populations. The highest powers in the capital have always had to contend with local power centers. The most successful Afghan rulers have found ways to control, co-opt, or otherwise work with tribal or regional leaders. In the end, all politics in Afghanistan is local in extremis.

Finally, by the ironies of fate, Afghanistan has always stood between contending powers, whether they came from Arabia, Iran, Russia, Great Britain, al Qaeda, the United States, or even India and Pakistan. Greeks, Persians, Arabs, and Mongols—Genghis Khan, Timur, Babur—as well as the British Raj, have had a turn at making war in Afghanistan. It is not true that Afghanistan has never been conquered. It is, however, accurate to note that the physical conquest of Afghanistan has often brought only a temporary Pyrrhic victory. National security policy has often had to contend with the situation described by "the Iron Amir," Abdur Rahman Khan, who ruled Afghanistan from 1880 to 1901:

How can a small power like Afghanistan, which is like a goat between these lions, or a grain of wheat between these two strong millstones of the grinding mill, stand in the midway of the stones without being crushed to death?[8]

2. The Struggle for Independence, Modernization, and Development

Afghanistan became a unified entity in the mid-1700s, a poor and underdeveloped country in a very rough neighborhood. Its size, shape, and degree of centralized power depended on leaders who, like President Karzai, were often from the Durrani confederation of southern Pashtuns, and whose biggest and toughest rivals were often the Ghilzai, or eastern Pashtuns, who were famous for their rebelliousness and martial spirit.[1] Beginning in the 1830s, Afghanistan fought two wars over the issue of Russia's feeble attempts at gaining influence and using Afghanistan against British India, which contained the territory of what is now modern Pakistan. The Third Anglo-Afghan War was fought after World War I for independence from British interference with Afghan affairs. This competition was referred to as the "Great Game," and some writers extend the term to cover any great power competition that involves Afghanistan.

The First Anglo-Afghan War, 1839–1842, was about blocking the Russian influence from the Indian border and extending British influence into Central Asia. The war began with a massive British invasion, the toppling of ruler Dost Mohammad, and an occupation of Kabul and other cities. After the British political agent was assassinated, the remnants of the first British expeditionary force (16,000 soldiers, dependents, and camp followers) tried to retreat back into India.[2] They were nearly all killed or dispersed, save for a lone regimental surgeon who returned home to tell the tale. The subsequent British punitive expedition killed thousands of Afghans and destroyed three cities, including Kabul. The British then withdrew. Dost Mohammad again became the ruler—called shah or emir (or amir) in different eras—and spent the remainder of his reign consolidating power, usually with a British subsidy.

In the Second Anglo-Afghan War, 1878–1880, disputes over potential Russian influence on Kabul again produced a British ultimatum, a rapid and successful invasion, a troubled occupation, a murdered British envoy, and subsequent maneuver warfare. Abdur Rahman became emir after a Pyrrhic victory for Great Britain. He pursued, in Barnett Rubin's phrase, "a coercion-intensive path to state formation" and ruled from the center with an iron fist (and significant British subsidies) until his death in 1901.[3] Rahman brought the country together and ruled well but harshly. He was forced to accept the hated Durand Line drawn by the British envoy, Sir Henry Mortimer Durand, to divide Afghanistan from India. It also divided the Pashtuns, leaving a third of them in Afghanistan and two-thirds in western India, which later became modern Pakistan. The results of the first two wars with Britain were longstanding Afghan-British tensions, an increase in Afghanistan's xenophobia, and an unresolved issue over the homeland of the Pashtuns, which was split between two countries.

In the first two Anglo-Afghan wars, the Afghans earned a well-justified reputation as fierce fighters with a taste for sometimes no-holds-barred battlefield behaviors and atrocities. Kipling allowed how no sane British soldier would ever let himself be captured even if wounded. His famous poem on basic soldiering gave new soldiers a grisly prescription:

If your officer's dead and the sergeants look white,
Remember it's ruin to run from a fight:
So take open order, lie down, and sit tight,

And wait for supports like a soldier.
Wait, wait, wait like a soldier. . . .

When you're wounded and left on Afghanistan's plains,
And the women come out to cut up what remains,
Jest roll to your rifle and blow out your brains
An' go to your Gawd like a soldier.
Go, go, go like a soldier,
Go, go, go like a soldier,
Go, go, go like a soldier,
So-oldier of the Queen![4]

Interestingly, the Afghan leaders fought against British encroachment, but then after besting or severely vexing the British to establish that independence, often ended up taking subsidies from them. The British in return received control over Afghan foreign policy. The subsidies were generally used to strengthen the Afghan army and further the internal power of the central government in Kabul. This rather stable situation continued until 1919, when a third Anglo-Afghan war, discussed below, won total independence. In a great political paradox, Afghan rulers were strongest within their nation when they were supported by foreign subsidies. Low or no subsidies meant taxing the locals and, at times, harsh conscription. These measures were never popular. The people were eager to salute the national rulers but not eager to have them interfere with local autonomy.

The Third Anglo-Afghan War followed World War I and established full independence. It began with the mysterious death of the old emir, Habibullah, who did not want another war with Britain because it had paid him a healthy subsidy. He had ruled peacefully for nearly two decades and kept Afghanistan neutral during the First World War. According to some historians, the new emir, Amanullah—a third son who seized power from those with stronger dynastic claims—was involved in his father's death.[5] He wanted a showdown with Great Britain. The Third Anglo-Afghan War involved very few battles, but the British did manage to use biplanes to bomb Jalalabad and Kabul. The war-weary British, however, soon gave in to Afghan demands for full independence. The war ended British subsidies—a key revenue source for Afghan leaders—and Great Britain's encroachment on Afghan sovereignty.

After victory in the third war, later celebrated as the beginning of Afghan self-rule, Amanullah decided to modernize his kingdom. He was the first Afghan ruler to take aid and military assistance from the Soviet Union. He announced reforms and predictably had to put down a few revolts in the east over taxation, conscription, and social changes, such as the education of women. A few years later, after retreating on his most objectionable reforms, Amanullah toured Europe for a few months. In 1928, he returned with a notion of becoming an Afghan version of Kemal Attaturk, the leader who made Turkey a modern secular state. Amanullah again pursued what were drastic reforms by Afghan standards, despite the fact that his previous attempts at reform had sparked a revolt in the east. This time he went further by removing the veil from women, pushing coeducation, and forcing Afghans to wear Western-style clothing in the capital. He alienated the conservative clergy, including those who had previously supported his modernization program.

A revolt, the Civil War of 1929,[6] broke out, the weakened king abdicated, and for 9 months a chaotic Afghanistan was ruled by Habibullah Kalakani (also referred to as Bacha Saqao, the "son of the water carrier"), seen by many as a Tajik brigand. Order returned with a reluctant Nadir Shah on the throne. He restored conservative rule only to be assassinated in 1933 by a young man seeking revenge for the death of a family member. Nadir Shah's dynasty, called Musahiban after the family name, ruled from 1929 to 1978.

After Nadir Shah's death, his teenage son, Zahir Shah, succeeded to the throne, although his paternal uncles ruled as regents until 1953. From 1953 to 1973, Zahir Shah ruled with various prime ministers, the first of which was his cousin, Prince Mohammed Daoud. During Zahir Shah's reign, Afghanistan managed to remain neutral in World War II, began to develop economically with the help of foreign aid, created a modern military with the help of the USSR, and stayed at an uneasy peace with its neighbors. Trouble with the new state of Pakistan, home to more than twice as many Pashtuns as Afghanistan, was a near constant. The Durand Line was always an issue, and from time to time the status of "Pashtunistan" was formally placed on the table by Afghan nationalists who demanded a plebiscite. Afghanistan even cast the only vote against Pakistan being admitted to the United Nations in 1947.

For its part, the United States did provide aid but in general was much less interested in Afghanistan than the Soviet Union was. Quotes often appeared in Embassy reports to Washington, such as:

For the United States, Afghanistan has at present limited direct interest: it is not an important trading partner . . . not an access route for U.S. trade with others . . . not a source of oil or scarce strategic metals . . . there are no treaty ties or defense commitments; and Afghanistan does not provide us with significant defense, intelligence, or scientific facilities. United States policy has long recognized these facts.[7]

Afghanistan was much more important for the Soviet Union. It was a neutral, developing state on the periphery of the USSR, beholden to Moscow for economic and military aid which was generously applied, especially in the early 1970s.

Daoud, the king's cousin, served as prime minister from 1953 until the start of the constitutional monarchy in 1964, which ended his term. The king chafed under the tutelage of his cousin and had it written into the constitution that no relative of the king could be a government minister. The constitutional monarchy—a half-hearted attempt at democracy with a parliament but no political parties—lasted about a decade until 1973, when the spurned Daoud, with the help of leftist army officers, launched a bloodless coup while Zahir Shah was abroad. Five years later, Daoud, who some inaccurately called "the Red Prince," was himself toppled in a coup by the leftists on whom he had turned his back. Another cycle of rapid and fruitless modernization efforts followed, accompanied by an unusually high amount of repression. The new and more radical heirs of Amanullah were avowed communists, completely bereft of common sense and out of touch with their own people. Their power base was found among disaffected eastern Pashtun intellectuals and Soviet-trained army officers.

A number of threads tie together the events of Afghan history in the time between Abdur Rahman's passing (1901) and the advent of the People's Democratic Party of Afghanistan (1978). They continue to exist today, woven into a contemporary context dominated by war, terrorism, globalization, radical Islam, and the information age. First, Afghanistan was in drastic need of modernization, but radical modernizers like Amanullah and the communists easily ran afoul of entrenched interests and a very conservative populace in the countryside that jealously guarded its autonomy. Afghan leaders in Kabul have usually had enormous formal power, but their direct rule has usually extended only to the Kabul area and the environs of the five major cities. A successful Afghan emir or president must learn to share power and deal effectively with local leaders.

Second, because of the perceived need to modernize, Afghanistan's intellectuals were awash with new ideas, some moderately Western, some leftist (encouraged by close relations with the Soviet Union), and some Islamist, although that group was small until the jihad against the Soviet Union increased its strength. Islam became the ideology of the jihad against the USSR, increasing in influence as the war progressed, and then again when the Taliban came to power. During this same period, Pakistan, home to four million Afghan refugees, was undergoing its own Islamization, first under General and President Zia ul Haq, and later his successors. Pakistani Islamization no doubt also influenced the fervor of Afghan refugees. Pakistani intelligence favored the fundamentalist Pashtun groups among the seven major Afghan resistance groups in the war against the Soviet Union.

Third, Afghanistan has often been politically unstable. Most of its 20th-century rulers were ousted or else killed in office or shortly after they left. To review: Abdur Rahman, the Iron Emir, died in office in 1901 and was succeeded by his son and designated heir, Habibullah. As Barnett Rubin wrote, "[His] peaceful succession was an event with no precedent and so far, no sequel."[8] Habibullah ruled for nearly two decades before he was assassinated on a hunting trip in 1919 under mysterious circumstances. Amanullah, his son, was ousted in 1929 for his efforts to rapidly modernize the country. Habibullah Kalakani, a Tajik, ruled for less than 9 months and was later executed. Next, Nadir Shah, a distant cousin of Amanullah, was offered the throne by an assembly of leaders. He returned to conservative Afghan principles on women's rights and sharia law but was assassinated 4 years later in 1933. Zahir Shah ruled from 1933 to 1973 until he was toppled in a coup by his cousin, Prince Daoud (prime minister from 1953 to 1963 and president from 1973 to 1978). In turn, Daoud and his family were later killed by Afghan communists in the 1978 coup. Three of the next four communist rulers (Taraki, Amin, and Najibullah) would be killed in or shortly after they left office. Only Babrak Karmal would survive after being ousted in 1986 and then exiled. Burhanuddin Rabbani succeeded Najibullah, but he was ousted by the Taliban. President Karzai's 12 predecessors have led tough lives: all of them have been forced from office, with seven being killed in the process. Still, the periods 1901–1919 and 1933–1973 were times of relative stability, proof positive that good governance in Afghanistan is problematical but not impossible. Instability has been common but is in no sense preordained.

Fourth, most of the rulers of Afghanistan faced "center versus periphery" issues that tended to generate internal conflicts. The intrusion of central power deep into the countryside resulted in many revolts against Amanullah, Daoud, and the four leaders of the People's Democratic Party of Afghanistan (PDPA): Taraki, Amin, Karmal, and Najibullah. Overlaid on many of these center-periphery debates were rivalries for the throne as well as tension between southern Pashtuns and their eastern cousins. Again, interference with the people's land, treasure, or women would be perceived as issues in many of the well-intentioned reforms. Alongside the modernization problem, Afghan rulers have usually been short on revenue. Foreign aid was often needed for regime security and basic population control. Many rulers have had to balance the tension between aid or subsidies on the one hand, and a strong desire for independence on the other.

Fifth, Afghans are superb fighters. Long experience fighting conventional armies and other tribes has made them expert warriors. Professor Larry Goodson has written that the Afghans were:

> *fiercely uncompromising warriors who excelled at political duplicity and guerrilla warfare. They mastered mobile hit and run and ambush tactics and understood the importance of seasonal warfare and tribal alliances against a common enemy. They were comfortable fighting on the rugged terrain . . . and aware how difficult it was for an invading army far from its home territory to effectively prosecute a protracted guerrilla war.*[9]

Finally, external pressures from great powers had significant effects. Whether contending with Iran and Pakistan, fighting the Soviet Union or Great Britain, or navigating the shoals of foreign aid from various suppliers, conflict and security tensions have been a hallmark of Afghan history. These international pressures and invaders have generated a widespread xenophobia that exists alongside the Afghans' well-deserved reputation for hospitality. A leader who rails against foreign influence is playing to a broad constituency. Afghanistan's internal and international conflicts have also been the enemy of development and tranquility, and the people continue to pay a high price.

3. The Saur "Revolution" and the Soviet-Afghan War, 1978–1989

The relative stability of 1933 to 1978 gave way to insurrection, first against Afghan communists and later the invading Soviet Union. The communist coup and the Soviet invasion touched off 33 years of war that continues to the present.

In 1978, as President Daoud's regime approached its fifth year, he realized that the leftists had grown strong during his rule. He began to tack to the right, warming to the United States while relations with Moscow cooled. A demonstration after the mysterious death of an Afghan leftist alarmed Daoud, who put the leading members of the People's Democratic Party of Afghanistan under house arrest. The leaders of that party called for a coup. A relatively small band of leftist army officers, with some logistical help from Soviet advisors, attacked the palace, killing Daoud and his family. The Saur (April) Revolution, an urban coup d'état, marked the birth of the Democratic Republic of Afghanistan.[1]

The PDPA was one party with two very different factions. The Khalq (Masses) faction, with great strength in the security services, was led by Nur Mohammad Taraki and Hafizullah Amin. A more moderate and broad-based group, the Parcham (Banner) faction, was led by Babrak Karmal. That party was soon pushed aside and its leader was sent abroad on ambassadorial duties. The leaders of the Khalq faction, Taraki and Amin were radical ideologues with a penchant for rapid modernization.

Their program—formed over Soviet objections—seemed almost designed to bring about an insurrection. Its main features were land reform, usury reform, and equal rights for women. All of these were unpopular. Land reform was particularly destabilizing. It was brutally applied and was most unpopular among peasants, who saw it as immoral and inconsistent with Islam. On top of all of this, the PDPA changed the national flag's color from Islamic green to socialist red. Caught somewhat by surprise, Moscow was publicly enthusiastic about the prospects for the new regime but concerned that the PDPA was alienating the people. They urged the PDPA to go slow at every turn. Soviet theorists were privately scornful of a socialist revolution in what they viewed as a feudal state.

After the coup, PDPA relations with the United States were generally correct but not very productive. Washington was concerned about the regime and its open penetration by Soviet advisors but even more worried about developments in neighboring Iran. In February 1979, U.S.-Afghan relations nosedived when radicals in Kabul kidnapped U.S. Ambassador Adolph "Spike" Dubs. Against American advice, a sloppy, Afghan-led, Soviet-advised rescue attempt ended up killing the kidnappers and the Ambassador. U.S. aid programs ended and the diplomatic profile was reduced.

At the same time, Afghanistan's conscripted army was unstable and not up to dealing with emerging mujahideen (holy warriors). Tensions between Soviet advisors and Afghan commanders also grew. In March 1979, the insurgency took a drastic turn. A rebel attack against the city of Herat, coupled with an army mutiny, resulted in the massacre of 50 Soviet officers and their dependents. Patrick Garrity wrote in 1980:

> Soviet advisors were hunted down by specially assigned insurgent assassination squads. . . . Westerners reportedly saw Russian women and children running for their lives from the area of the Soviet-built Herat Hotel. Those Russians that were caught were killed: some were flayed alive, others were beheaded and cut into pieces.[2]

A leading figure in the attack on the Soviet advisors was then–Afghan army Captain Ismail Khan, who later became a resistance leader and then a regional warlord (who preferred the title emir), and thereafter a Karzai cabinet officer.

The Kremlin was quite concerned. After lengthy debate, however, Politburo principals rejected the use of the Soviet army. Yuri Andropov, a former KGB head and future Soviet leader, gave his reasoning against using Soviet troops: "We can suppress a revolution in Afghanistan only with the aid of our bayonets, and that is for us entirely inadmissible." Foreign Minister Andrei Gromyko agreed and noted that other advances with the United States and Europe would be put in jeopardy by using force.[3]

The Afghan army conducted retaliation attacks in Herat, and Moscow beefed up its advisory efforts. Throughout 1979, Soviet advisors came to be found at nearly every echelon. Soviet pilots flew combat missions. A succession of Soviet generals conducted assessments that resulted in increases in advisors and equipment. Senior Soviet generals, however, were steadfast in their opposition to sending in a Soviet expeditionary force. They were keenly aware that this would inflame the situation and that their formations were tailored for conventional war on the plains of Europe, not for counterinsurgency in the Afghan mountains. The Soviet leadership agreed with this assessment until the fall of 1979.[4]

President Taraki visited Moscow in September 1979. He was told by the Soviet leadership that he had to moderate his program and that the major obstacle to change was his power hungry, radical prime minister, Hafizullah Amin. Taraki hatched a plot, but Amin learned of it and countered with one of his own. Shortly after a photo of Taraki embracing Brezhnev appeared on the front of *Pravda*, Taraki was killed by Amin's henchmen. Amin then took the positions of defense secretary, prime minister, president, and general secretary of the party.

The Soviet Union's position of strength in Afghanistan was eroding, opening the Central Asian Republics to possible contagion from radical Islamists there. It appeared to Moscow that Washington might go to war to rescue its hostages in Iran. Hafizullah Amin had shamed the Soviet leadership, and the military situation was spiraling out of control. The Soviet leadership also believed that Amin had begun to reach out to the United States for help. Soviet-American relations were at a low point. Despite Gromyko's sentiments months before, there were no prospective political benefits from the United States—already angry at Soviet aggressiveness in the Third World—that would deter the Soviet Union from using the stick.

The debilitated Soviet leader, Leonid Brezhnev, and a group of fewer than a half dozen Politburo members decided that the situation had to be stabilized and then repaired. They ordered an invasion over the objections of the chief of the general staff.

A post-decisional Central Committee memorandum signed by Andropov, Gromyko, and others made the case for the invasion. It accused Amin of "murder," establishing a "personal dictatorship . . . smearing the Soviet Union," and making efforts "to mend relations with America . . . [by holding] a series of meetings with the American charge d'affaires in Kabul." They also accused Amin of attempting to reach "a compromise with leaders of the internal counter-revolution."[5] Based on these events and the perceived requirements of the Soviet-Afghan Friendship Treaty, the senior Politburo members wrote, "a decision has been made to send the necessary contingent of the Soviet army to Afghanistan." The intent of the Soviet military operation was to unseat Amin and his close associates, install the pliable Babrak Karmal as president, show the flag in the countryside, and hold the cities and lines of communication until the Afghan security forces could be rebuilt. Soviet intentions proved the validity of the old folk wisdom: there's many a slip between the cup and the lip.

All of this came at the end of 1979, a time of great change in international relations. The Shah of Iran was overthrown and U.S. diplomats were later taken hostage by the radical regime in Tehran. Israel and Egypt signed the Camp David Accords, marking the high-water mark of U.S. influence in what had once been a Soviet ally. Islamist radicals seized the Grand Mosque in Mecca but failed to bring down the monarchy there. A Pakistani mob, misguided by rumors of U.S. involvement in the seizure of the mosque, burned the American Embassy in Islamabad. Finally, the December invasion of Afghanistan by the Soviet Union added great stress to superpower relations. It was the first time the Soviet Union used its own forces to attack a nation outside the Warsaw Pact. This drastic violation of Cold War expectations resulted in a proxy war between the superpowers.[6]

The Soviet invasion in late December 1979 was a well-executed operation. Previously infiltrated commandos moved on the palace and killed Amin and his entourage. Paratroopers seized bases in and around the capital. Two motorized rifle divisions filled with reservists from the Central Asia Republics—one from Termez in the north central region and one from Kushka, Turkmenistan, in the west—brought the number of Soviet troops to 50,000 by the end of the first week of January 1980. Over time, the reservists would be withdrawn and the Soviet force increased to 130,000.[7]

Karmal was not successful in unifying the government. Afghan army forces that did not desert continued to perform poorly, just as the resistance—energized by the invasion—moved into high gear. Soviet forces were not trained for counterinsurgency and, lacking recent experience in mountain warfare, did not perform well in the Afghan environment. Later, the Soviets would move in large-scale operations to clear areas of strong mujahideen elements. They rarely held areas in the countryside and never tried to govern them systematically. They did not see their mission as protecting the population, nor did they exercise great care regarding civilian casualties and collateral damage. Afghan refugees increased, along with international outrage.

Soviet military efforts were hampered by slow learning within the Soviet armed forces. It would take 5 years before they began agile strike operations with air assault and airborne forces. A second problem was international isolation and significant support for the insurgents. The invasion of Afghanistan was a heinous act, and even East European and Cuban communists were slow to help. China and the United States kept up a drumbeat of criticism. Washington instituted a grain embargo and boycotted the Moscow Olympics. Moreover, Pakistan, Saudi Arabia, and the United States, usually working through Pakistani intelligence, came to the aid of the mujahideen, who maintained sanctuaries in Pakistan. During the second Reagan administration, the mujahideen were provided with shoulder-fired antiaircraft missiles, which took a serious toll on Soviet aircraft. At its height, U.S. aid to the mujahideen, nearly all distributed by Pakistan's Inter-Services Intelligence (ISI) directorate, rose to $400 million per year.[8]

The deck was stacked against the Soviet military effort. As an avowedly atheist foreign power, it had allied itself with a hated regime completely out of step with the Afghan people. The government had little legitimacy. The military tasks were daunting and the Karmal government had little international support outside the Soviet Union. It had too few soldiers to control the countryside, so they limited themselves to sweeps or clearing operations. The enemy had a secure sanctuary and great amounts of international support. A contemporary account noted that:

> *To date, Soviet strategy appears to have been to hold the major centers of communications, limit infiltration, and destroy local strongholds at minimum costs to their own forces. In essence, the Soviet strategy [was] one wherein high technology, superior tactical mobility, and firepower are used to make up for an insufficient number of troops and to hold Soviet casualties to a minimum. In effect, Soviet policy seems to be a combination of scorched earth and migratory genocide.*[9]

A new age dawned in the Soviet Union in 1985. Mikhail Gorbachev, a Communist reformer, became general secretary of the Communist Party of the Soviet Union and leader of the tottering Soviet regime, which had buried three of its previous rulers in as many years. A dedicated communist, he set out to unleash his program of new thinking, democratization, openness, and restructuring on a Soviet Union that found it to be very strong medicine. The war in Afghanistan fit Gorbachev's transformational agenda, to borrow Stalin's phrase, "like a saddle fits a cow."

The Soviet Union moved quickly to shore up Afghan leadership. In 1986, the increasingly ineffective Karmal was relieved, and the young and dynamic Najibullah—a one-time medical student and the former head of the Secret Police—was put in his place. While Najibullah tried to remove the communist taint from his government, he rebuilt the army, changed the name of the governing party, and formed alliances with local militias. He was not a man of scruples, but he was clever and got things done.

Gorbachev apparently gave the Soviet army a year to fight on in Afghanistan, provided extra resources, and encouraged its experimentation. The USSR pushed the reform of the Afghan army, and the Soviet advisors and Najibullah's cadres were quite successful in their last few years at building the Afghan army and organizing friendly militia groups.

With the stalemate continuing, Gorbachev proceeded to negotiate first a withdrawal of Soviet forces, which was completed in February 1989, and then—along with his successors—an ineffective bilateral cut-off of military aid to all combatants. Most people thought those actions would soon bring an end to the war. They were wrong. Najibullah was able to continue fighting for 3 years after the Soviet departure. His regime, however, vanished shortly after the Soviet Union disappeared as a state. Najibullah left the field in 1992 but was unable to escape. The civil war continued after Najibullah's departure, first among the so-called Peshawar Seven groups[10] and then between those groups and the Taliban.

Before moving to the civil war and beyond, it is important to deal with a common misperception. Some pundits, both American and Russian, see the United States today in the same boat in Afghanistan as the USSR was in the 1980s, a second superpower bogged down in the "graveyard of empires" and destined to meet the same fate.[11] This label overestimates the effects of defeats on Great Britain and the Soviet Union. While the "graveyard of empires" is an important warning, it should not be taken as a literal prediction for the United States and its coalition partners.[12] There are many surface parallels and potential lessons, but the Soviet and American policy and operations in Afghanistan were essentially different.[13]

The United States is a superpower, but it is not an empire. It does not need to occupy countries or replicate American governmental structures or political ideology to accomplish its long-term goals. In Afghanistan, after having been attacked by resident terrorists, the United States came to the aid of combatants fighting an unpopular government recognized by only three countries. American forces did not kill any U.S. allies and replace them with puppets during the invasion. The Soviets forced over four million Afghans into exile, while the United States created conditions where the vast majority of them have returned.

In one sense, both Washington and Moscow were unprepared for a protracted insurgency in Afghanistan. The Soviet Union, however, fought with punishing fury in the countryside. War crimes and illegal punitive operations were daily occurrences. There was no talk about protecting the population; Soviet operations were all about protecting the regime and furthering Soviet control. Today, the United States has in large measure adapted to the insurgency and is working hard to protect the people, who are being besieged by the lawless Taliban, itself a purveyor of war crimes and human rights violations.

The Soviet army's enemy in Afghanistan was the whole nation; the United States and its coalition partners—49 of them in 2010—are fighting an extremist religious minority group of no more than 25,000 to 35,000 fighters whose national popularity rarely rises above 10 percent.[14] Finally, the Soviet Union fought to secure an authoritarian state with an alien ideology, while the United States and its allies are trying to build a stable state with democratic aspirations where people have basic freedoms and a claim on prosperity. Even in its beleaguered condition, the Karzai regime—twice elected nationwide—has far more legitimacy than the Afghan communists ever did. Beyond the locale, the importance of sanctuaries, and the great power status of the United States and the Soviet Union, there are not a lot of similarities between Moscow's conflict and the war being fought by the United States and its coalition partners.

In the end, the Soviet experience in Afghanistan cost 15,000 Soviet and a million Afghan lives, created a huge Afghan diaspora, left tens of millions of mines on the ground, and hastened the demise of the Soviet Union. Sadly, it did not create a better peace. In fact, it did not create any peace. After the departure of the Soviet Union in 1989, a civil war would continue to the start of the next century, first against the Najibullah regime, then among the mujahideen groups, and then between those groups and the upstart Taliban. After the Taliban seized Kabul in the fall of 1996, it continued to fight the non-Pashtun mujahideen, who reorganized as the Northern Alliance.

4. Civil War and Advent of the Taliban

While many expected the departure of the Soviet army in February 1989 to mark the end of the war, it did not. The Najibullah regime—aided by Soviet security assistance—was clever and built alliances around the country. With a 65,000-man army, an air force of nearly 200 planes and helicopters, and many well-paid militia units, Afghan government forces were able to hold off the mujahideen. This fact became clear in May 1989, when a number of mujahideen groups attacked, but failed to seize, the city of Jalalabad in eastern Afghanistan. The army was simply a better and more cohesive force than the fractious insurgents were. The disparate mujahideen groups—dubbed the Peshawar Seven—failed to cooperate and often fought viciously among themselves. Najibullah was well supported by the Soviet Union and fought effectively for 3 years. In March 1992, lacking foreign supporters after the demise of the Soviet Union, Najibullah stopped fighting, but he was unable to leave the country and took refuge in the UN Compound where he remained until seized by the Taliban in 1996.[1]

Civil Wars: 1992–1996

In 1992, with UN help, a provisional government was formed to rule the country. It failed because of infighting among the mujahideen. The conflict was particularly bitter between the eastern Pashtun, Hezb-i-Islami followers of Gulbuddin Hekmatyar, who were supported by Pakistan, and the Tajik fighters of Ahmed Shah Massoud's Jamiat-i-Islami, who came to control Kabul. Burhanuddin Rabbani, a Tajik and the political head of the Jamiat-i-Islami group, was ultimately named president; Gulbuddin Hekmatyar was designated prime minister of the interim government; and Ahmed Shah Massoud was selected as defense minister. Sadly, the government never met at the conference table, only on the urban battlefield.

The civil war featured fierce fighting over Kabul—occupied by Massoud but desired by Hekmatyar, his archrival—and in some other major cities, which to that point had escaped most active combat. From April 1992 to April 1993, much of Kabul was destroyed and 30,000 inhabitants were killed, with another 100,000 wounded.[2] In other cities, things were often more peaceful under the control of local warlords, such as Ismail Khan in Herat and Abdul Rashid Dostum in Mazar-i-Sharif. In many other places, however, law and order disintegrated. Local or regional warlords were dominant and men with guns made the rules. In Kandahar and other locations, rape, armed robbery, kidnapping young boys, and other crimes of violence were all too common.

Fearing the instability growing in Afghanistan, and disenchanted with the mujahideen groups it had assisted since 1980, the Pakistani government began to slowly withdraw its support from them in 1994 in favor of Afghan and Pakistani madrassa graduates called the Taliban, a group focused on sharia-based law and order. The leaders of these students were radical Islamists, many of whom were self-educated holy men. While zealous and often devout, there were no great Koranic scholars or religious thinkers among them, nor were there many engineers, physicians, or experienced government bureaucrats. Taliban leaders often supplanted Pashtun tribal leaders. They were led by Mullah Mohammad Omar Akhund (also known as Mullah Mohammad Omar Mujahid, or simply Mullah Omar), a country cleric from Kandahar and a former anti-Soviet resistance commander who had lost an eye in battle. His deputies included many wounded veterans of the war with the Soviet Union.

After a few small-scale local successes in the Kandahar region, a Taliban field force with modern weaponry emerged from Pakistan, first operating around Kandahar and then nationwide. They drew on recruits from extremist madaris—Islamic schools—in Pakistan, and those located from Ghazni to Kandahar in southern Afghanistan. Ahmed Rashid's and Anthony Davis's research confirm that in Spin Boldak (adjacent to the Pakistani province of Baluchistan), the Taliban seized "some 18,000 Kalashnikovs, dozens of artillery pieces, large quantities of ammunition, and many vehicles" that belonged to Pakistan's ISI and were being guarded by fighters from the Hezb-i-Islami group.[3] Martin Ewans, a former British diplomat, reported:

> *The Taliban forces that proceeded to advance through Afghanistan in the winter of 1994–95 were equipped with tanks, APCs, artillery, and even aircraft, but however much equipment they may have acquired in Spin Boldak, Kandahar or elsewhere, they could not despite energetic denials, have operated without training, ammunition, fuel, and maintenance facilities provided by Pakistan. . . . Within no more than six months, they had mobilized possibly as many as 20,000 fighting men . . . many [of whom] were Pakistanis.*[4]

With Pakistani advice and armaments, the unified Taliban sliced through the outlaw gunmen and contending mujahideen groups with great alacrity. In 1994, they took Kandahar and then other major cities. In 1996, the disintegrating Rabbani regime lost Kabul to the Taliban, aided by the defections of Gulbuddin Hekmatyar and Jalaluddin Haqqani, who ended up allied with the Taliban. In September 1996, the Taliban took

37

Najibullah and his brother from the UN Compound, tortured and killed them, dragged their bodies behind vehicles, and then hung the pair on a lamppost near the Presidential Palace.[5] Commander Massoud made an orderly retreat to the north, where he was later joined by Hazara fighters and Uzbeks under Commander Dostum.

The Taliban pursued and took Mazar-i-Sharif, lost it, and seized it again. On the Taliban's second capture in 1998, seeking revenge for past massacres against its own cadres, its forces massacred Hazara defenders and also killed Iranian diplomats, causing an international crisis that drove a deep divide between the Sunni Taliban and the Shia regime in Tehran. In all, the new Northern Alliance of Tajik, Uzbek, and Hazara fighters never occupied more than 15–20 percent of the countryside.[6] The Taliban, aided by al Qaeda–trained Afghan and foreign cadres, kept up pressure on the Northern Alliance until 2001.

The Taliban set up its capital in Kabul and appointed ministers, but the command element remained in Kandahar with Mullah Omar. It often contradicted Kabul's repressive and at times ludicrous government. Clever with religious symbols, Mullah Omar literally put on the cloak of the Prophet Mohammad, which was kept in a Kandahar shrine, and proclaimed himself *Amir-ul-Mominin*, Commander of the Faithful, raising his status among even the most radical extremists. Al Qaeda seniors and the Pakistani Taliban have always accorded Mullah Omar great respect and acknowledge him with his self-awarded title. The Taliban regime was recognized as legitimate by only three nations: Pakistan, the United Arab Emirates, and Saudi Arabia, though the latter two maintained only a limited diplomatic presence in Kabul. The United States and United Nations continued to give aid to the people, but Afghanistan's seat at the United Nations and most embassies abroad remained occupied by representatives of the previous regime led by Rabbani.

The Rule of the Taliban

Having taken control of the country and implemented sharia-based law and order, the Taliban appeared to be puzzled by how to run the government or manage the economy, which went from bad to worse, especially when UN sanctions for narcotics trafficking and droughts were added to the mix. Public health, in part because of Taliban-imposed restrictions on the mobility of female midwives, declined markedly. These failures were intimately connected to the Taliban itself and what they practiced. They generally opposed progress and modernity. French scholar Olivier Roy noted:

> *The men who formed the original core of the Taliban had learned and imparted a version of Islam that differed significantly from other fundamentalists. . . . [The] Madrassa education instilled in Pakistan focused on returning Afghan society to an imagined pre-modern period in which a purer form of Islam was practiced by a more righteous Muslim society. This made the Taliban approach to governance somewhat utopian in its attempt to battle the enemies of modernity and non-orthodoxy.*[7]

In light of these leanings, the Taliban victory decrees were understandable and even predictable. On taking Kabul, the Taliban's decrees were among the most repressive public policy decrees ever issued. Here are their cardinal elements:

- ✦ prohibition against female exposure [or being outside without burka and male relative]
- ✦ prohibition against music

✦ prohibition against shaving

✦ mandatory prayer

✦ prohibition against the rearing of pigeons and bird fighting

✦ eradication of narcotics and the users thereof

✦ prohibition against kite flying

✦ prohibition against the reproduction of pictures

✦ prohibition against gambling

✦ prohibition against British and American hairstyles

✦ prohibition on interest on loans, exchange charges, and charges on transactions

✦ prohibition against [women] washing clothes by the river embankments

✦ prohibition against music and dancing at weddings

✦ prohibition against playing drums

✦ prohibition against [male] tailors sewing women's clothes or taking measurements of women

✦ prohibition against witchcraft.[8]

The Ministry for the Promotion of Virtue and the Extermination of Sin was quite active. Women who disobeyed the directives could be beaten by the religious police. Public executions for serious criminals or adulterers were well publicized. The Taliban forced women to wear the *burka*, or as it is more commonly called in Afghanistan, the *chadari*, a one-piece body covering where women looked out at the world through a slit or a four-by-six-inch piece of mesh sewn into the headpiece. The Taliban's measures annoyed many Afghans, especially in the urban areas where life had been traditionally less restrictive.

In addition to human rights violations, the Taliban declared war on art, no doubt aided by their ascetic brethren in al Qaeda, who had similar puritanical beliefs. Thousands of books were burned. The national museum in Kabul, the repository of many pre-Islamic relics and works of art, was systematically vandalized by Taliban operatives eager to rid Afghanistan of the graven images of its past. The possession of Western-style fashion magazines became a crime. Works of art or history books showing human faces or female forms were destroyed. The animals in the Kabul Zoo were tortured or killed by Taliban rank and file. Only a few specimens, including a blind lion and a bear whose nose had been cut off by a Talib, survived to 2001.[9] At the height of this fervor, against the objections of the UN and many nations, the Taliban destroyed the Bamiyan Buddhas, two pre-Islamic, 6th century A.D. sandstone sculptures carved directly from a cliff—one 150 feet and the other 121 feet in height. The Taliban saw them as idols and not ancient works of art, a point with which their al Qaeda benefactors agreed.[10]

As heinous as their domestic policies were, the worst aspect of Taliban governance was its virtual adoption of the al Qaeda terrorist organization. Osama bin Laden came back to Afghanistan in 1996, shortly before the Taliban took Kabul. He had fought there with the mujahideen for short periods during the Soviet war. His duties had included a little fighting, much fund-raising in Pakistan, and the supervision of construction efforts.[11] After a few years at home, he was ousted first from Saudi Arabia in 1991 for objecting to the introduction of U.S. forces during the Gulf War, and then from Sudan in 1996 because he had become a threat to the regime. Neither country would put up with his revolutionary activities and radical ways.[12]

Osama bin Laden reportedly saw Afghanistan as the first state in a new Islamic caliphate. Although he did not know Mullah Omar beforehand, bin Laden held him in high regard, and intermarriage took place between the inner circles of al Qaeda and the Taliban.[13] In return for his sanctuary and freedom of action, bin Laden provided funds, advice, and, most important, trained cadres, Afghan or otherwise, for the Taliban war machine. Pakistan was also generous in support of its allies in Afghanistan, which it saw as a sure bulwark against Indian influence. In 1998 alone, Pakistan provided $6 million to the Taliban.[14]

In Afghanistan, bin Laden took over or set up training camps for al Qaeda and Taliban recruits. As many as 20,000 Afghan and foreign recruits may have passed through the camps.[15] Many of these trainees received combat experience in fighting the Northern Alliance, raising al Qaeda's value in the eyes of the Taliban leadership. Afghanistan became a prime destination for international terrorists. In February 1998, bin Laden declared war on the United States from his safe haven in Afghanistan. Accusing the Americans of occupying Arabia, plundering its riches, humiliating its leaders, attacking Iraq, and more, bin Laden claimed that de facto the United States had declared war on Islam and its people. In an allegedly binding fatwa, or religious finding, bin Laden and his cosigners declared a defensive jihad that (theoretically) all Muslims were required to participate in:

> *To kill Americans and their allies, both civil and military, is an individual duty of every Muslim who is able, in any country where this is possible, until the* [main mosques in Jerusalem and Mecca] *are freed from their grip, and until their armies, shattered and broken-winged, depart from all the lands of Islam, incapable of threatening any Muslim.*[16]

Further on, the fatwa exhorts "every Muslim . . . to kill the Americans and plunder their possessions wherever he finds them and whenever he can." Muslim leaders and soldiers were also directed to "launch attacks against the armies of the American devils" and their allies.[17]

On August 7, 1998, al Qaeda carried out bombings on the U.S. Embassies in Kenya and Tanzania in East Africa. Both Embassies were severely damaged. The casualties, mostly African, numbered over 220 killed, and nearly 4,200 wounded. Among other measures, U.S. retaliatory cruise missile strikes were aimed at al Qaeda camps in Afghanistan to little effect. The 9/11 Commission concluded that the strikes missed bin Laden by a few hours.[18] Before and after these attacks, a number of plots to capture or kill bin Laden were stillborn due to sensitivities about civilian casualties. In 1999, the 9/11 plotters received screening and initial training inside Afghanistan. Their guidance, funds, concept of the operation, and detailed plans came from al Qaeda central in Afghanistan. Beginning in 1998, the United States and Saudi Arabia both urged Afghanistan to surrender Osama bin Laden for legal proceedings. The Taliban government resisted repeated efforts to extradite him even after he had blown up two U.S. Embassies and, in October 2000, a U.S. warship off the coast of Yemen. To this day (2011), the Taliban leadership has never disavowed al Qaeda or Osama bin Laden.

By 2001, al Qaeda was a terrorist group with its own state. For reasons of money, ignorance, hospitality, ideology, or self-interest, Mullah Omar and the Taliban did not interfere with the activities of "the Arabs." The 9/11 Commission concluded that:

> *Through his relationship with Mullah Omar—and the monetary and other benefits that it brought the Taliban—Bin Ladin was*

able to circumvent restrictions; Mullah Omar would stand by him even when other Taliban leaders raised objections. . . . Al Qaeda members could travel freely within the country, enter or exit it without visas or any immigration procedures, purchase and import vehicles and weapons, and enjoy the use of official Afghan Ministry of Defense license plates. Al Qaeda also used the Afghan state-owned Ariana Airlines to courier money into the country.[19]

5. 9/11 and the War Against the Taliban Government

It is not clear what al Qaeda's leaders thought would happen in Afghanistan after the 9/11 attacks. Perhaps, judging from recent practice, al Qaeda thought the Bush administration, like some of its predecessors, would conduct a lengthy investigation and be slow to take action. The United States had failed to take significant retaliatory action after other terrorist attacks: the 1983 bombing of the Marine Barracks in Lebanon, the 1993 bombing of the World Trade Center, the 1996 Khobar Towers attack in Saudi Arabia, and the bombing of USS *Cole* in 2000. Other terrorists no doubt believed that the United States would strike with its airpower and cruise missiles, as it had done frequently in Iraq, and once in Afghanistan after the Embassy bombings in 1998. Realists among the terrorists might have believed that ultimately the United States would attack but that it would get bogged down just as the Soviet Union did. Others, after the fact, including Osama bin Laden, suggested that drawing the United States into the Middle Eastern and Central Asian wars and draining its power was an integral part of the al Qaeda strategy.[1]

In any case, al Qaeda did not fully understand the passions that they would raise in the United States and among its allies by the murder on 9/11 of 3,000 innocent people from 90 countries. Washington asked the Taliban to turn over bin Laden. Mullah Omar refused again as he had in 1998. The President then went to Congress for support. Congress authorized the President in a Joint Resolution:

> *To use all necessary and appropriate force against those nations,*
> *organizations, or persons he determines planned, authorized,*

committed, or aided the terrorist attacks that occurred on Sep-
tember 11, 2001, or harbored such organizations or persons, in
order to prevent any future acts of international terrorism against
the United States by such nations, organizations or persons.[2]

U.S. air attacks began on October 7, 2001. By month's end, CIA paramilitary and SOF teams had begun to operate with the Northern Alliance and friendly Pashtun tribes in the south. Pakistan was an anomalous feature in this war. Desirous of influence in Afghanistan, Pakistan had at first supported the more religious mujahideen groups, and then the Taliban. After 9/11, American officials, including Deputy Secretary of State Richard Armitage, gave senior Pakistani officials an alternative to either support America or to be at war against it. With great prodding, Pakistan came around, put pressure on the Afghan regime, and provided the United States the logistic space and facilities needed to go to war. This worked well at the time, but James Dobbins, the Bush administration's representative to the resistance and Special Envoy for the post-Taliban conferences, made a valuable observation about U.S. cooperation over the years with Pakistan:

This setup has proved a mixed blessing. While providing the
United States [in the 1980s] a conduit for guns and money, it
had allowed the Pakistanis to determine who received the aid. The
Pakistani Inter-Services Intelligence Directorate had tended to fa-
vor the most extreme and fundamentalist mujahidin groups. After
the Soviets' withdrawal in 1989, American assistance had ceased.
The ISI, however, continued to support the more religiously ex-
treme factions in Afghanistan and from among them fostered the

emergence of the Taliban. After 9/11 the American and Pakistani intelligence services found themselves suddenly aligned again, this time in seeking to overthrow the very regime the ISI had installed in Kabul. Many on the American side now questioned the sincerity of Pakistan's commitment to this new goal.[3]

For their part, the Pakistanis questioned America's short attention span, its strategic relationship with India, and its loyalty and reliability as an ally for the long haul. For many Pakistanis, the United States had betrayed them three times. The first two came when Washington failed to support them in their wars with India. The third was in October 1990, not long after the Soviet withdrawal from Afghanistan, when the United States under the Pressler Amendment stopped all aid to Pakistan over Islamabad's failure to live up to nonproliferation agreements. In light of these perceived betrayals, some Pakistanis asked how long Washington would remain allied after completion of a war against the Taliban regime in Afghanistan. How would helping the United States in Afghanistan impact Pakistan's existential competition with India? From a Pakistani perspective, it made perfect sense to hedge their bets on the future of Kabul. The Taliban was hard to work with, but it was a sure thing, while the United States was an extremely powerful but fickle ally.[4]

Operation *Enduring Freedom* has had two phases in its war in Afghanistan. The first—from October 2001 to March 2002—was an example of conventional fighting, and the second of an evolved insurgency. In the first phase, despite remarks about the "transformation of warfare" and Green Berets on horseback calling in precision-guided bombs "danger close," the initial phase of Operation *Enduring Freedom* was a conventional, network-centric military operation.[5] It featured the Northern Alliance—a united front of Tajiks, Hazarra, and Uzbeks—and anti-Taliban Pashtun forces fighting a war of maneuver against the Taliban and its foreign-fighter supporters, many of whom were trained in al Qaeda camps in Afghanistan. The U.S. contribution came in the form of airpower and advice from Special Operations Forces and the Central Intelligence Agency paramilitary personnel. The CIA had provided an important service before 9/11 by maintaining close relations with Massoud and his Northern Alliance. These CIA and SOF teams—approximately 500 warriors—also connected Northern Alliance and friendly Pashtun ground power to the awesome effects of American aircraft and UAVs. Secretary of Defense Donald Rumsfeld heralded the U.S. contribution:

> *On the appointed day, one of their teams slipped in and hid well behind the lines, ready to call in airstrikes, and the bomb blasts would be the signal for others to charge. When the moment came, they signaled their targets to the coalition aircraft and looked at their watches. Two minutes and 15 seconds, 10 seconds—and then, out of nowhere, precision-guided bombs began to land on Taliban and al-Qaeda positions. The explosions were deafening, and the timing so precise that, as the soldiers described it, hundreds of Afghan horsemen literally came riding out of the smoke, coming down on the enemy in clouds of dust and flying shrapnel. A few carried RPGs. Some had as little as 10 rounds for their weapons. And they rode boldly Americans, Afghans, towards the Taliban and al Qaeda fighters. It was the first cavalry attack of the 21st century. . . .*

Now, what won the battle for Mazar [in early November 2001] *and set in motion the Taliban's fall from power was a combination of ingenuity of the Special Forces, the most advanced precision-guided munitions in the U.S. arsenal delivered by U.S. Navy, Air Force and Marine crews, and the courage of the Afghan fighters. . . . That day on the plains of Afghanistan, the 19th century met the 21st century, and they defeated a dangerous and determined adversary, a remarkable achievement.*[6]

The last battle in the first phase, Operation *Anaconda*, was fraught with tactical difficulties, but it broke up a hardcore Taliban and al Qaeda strongpoint in the Shahi Kot valley, northwest of Khost.[7] It also exposed defects in unity of command, which were later corrected.

Overall, post-9/11, U.S. conventional operations were successful but not decisive. The United States neither destroyed the enemy nor its will to resist. The Taliban field forces were defeated, and the regime ousted, but Osama bin Laden, much of the leadership of al Qaeda, as many as 1,000 of its fighters, Mullah Omar, and much of the Taliban's senior leaders escaped to safe havens in Pakistan and other nearby countries.[8] For many radicals, the United States and its allies soon became a Western occupier of Islamic lands.

With help from the international community, the United Nations called a conference at Bonn, Germany.[9] The United States and its allies did not invite even the most moderate of the Taliban—and there were a few—to participate in the Bonn Process to establish a new government. In retrospect, this may have been a mistake, but it was understandable. No one was in a mood to sit down with the discredited allies of al Qaeda, who had covered themselves with human rights abuses and brought ruin down on themselves by supporting al Qaeda. As a result of the conference, Afghan leaders formed an interim government without Taliban participation. Hamid Karzai, a Durrani Pashtun, was appointed president. The powerful, Tajik-dominated Northern Alliance controlled the power ministries: Defense (Mohammad Fahim Khan), Interior (Yunus Qanooni), and Foreign Affairs (Abdullah Abdullah).[10] The United Nations Security Council has recognized the legitimacy of the government and renewed the ISAF mandate each year since the Bonn Accords.[11]

In Afghanistan in 2002, there were two salient conditions: it was socioeconomically in the bottom 10 countries in the world, and it had almost no human capital to build on. The international community soon pledged over $5 billion in aid and began the tough work of helping to rebuild a devastated country. The aid did not meet Afghanistan's needs. Compared to allied programs in Bosnia and Kosovo, per capita aid to Afghanistan the first few years was very low.[12] Aid donors and NGOs had to find ways of building up or working around a skeletal, low-performing interim Afghan government. The latter proved to be easier, but that caused another problem: the provision of assistance outpaced capacity-building. Afghanistan rapidly became dependent on aid that it did not control.

Early in 2002, with the help of the United States, the government created a new Afghan National Army (ANA), with a target of 70,000 troops. An international peacekeeping force, the International Security Assistance Force, at the start consisting of about 4,000 non-U.S. soldiers and airmen, secured the Kabul region, which included about 250 square miles of territory in and around the capital. The Bush administration had a limited appetite for nation-building and only wanted a small presence for counterterrorism and limited aid. Around 8,000 U.S. and allied troops—mostly based at either Bagram Airbase, north of Kabul, or near Kandahar—conducted counterterrorist operations across the country. Lead nations—the United States for the Afghan National Army, the British for counternarcotics, the Italians for the Justice sector, the Germans for police training, and the Japanese for disarmament, demobilization, and reintegration of combatants—moved out to help in their respective areas but at a very slow pace.

The U.S. Department of Defense did not want to talk about its efforts there as counterinsurgency. Some in the Bush administration were concerned specifically about limiting expectations for nation-building, which was not a Presidential priority in the first Bush administration, especially after its main focus shifted to preparation for war in Iraq. In all, the Bush administration was not in favor of using the U.S. Armed Forces in peacekeeping operations and long-term postconflict commitments. Over the years, the Bush team begrudgingly came to terms with the need for nation-building in Iraq and Afghanistan. In the latter, progress was slow but steady, and in the 3 years after the U.S. intervention the Taliban appeared to be relatively dormant. Kabul, which was guarded and patrolled by ISAF, remained reasonably calm. After more than two decades of war, many believed that peace had come to the Hindu Kush.

The Taliban and al Qaeda, however, had other plans. They intended to launch an insurgency to regain power in Kabul. Their hope was that the international community would tire of nation-building under pressure and would ultimately depart, leaving Karzai to the same horrible fate that befell Najibullah when they seized Kabul in 1996. The Taliban had sanctuaries in Pakistan in the Federally Administered Tribal Areas, the Northwest Frontier Province (Khyber Pakhtunkhwa), Baluchistan in Pakistan, and other countries. Other Taliban leaders found refuge among their coethnics in Karachi. The Taliban also had strong points in a number of Afghan provinces, such as Helmand, where there were few coalition or Afghan government forces until 2006. Along with the demise of the Taliban had come the rebirth of the narcotics industry, a mark of poverty but also an indicator of a new atmosphere of lawlessness. The Taliban, which had ended the cultivation of poppy in the last year of their reign, encouraged its rebirth and supported the movement with charity from the Gulf states, "taxes," and profits from the drug trade.

Given the U.S. record in Vietnam and Lebanon, as well as the recent U.S. response to terrorist incidents, the Taliban had some reason to believe that time was on their side. One familiar saying epitomized their approach: "the Americans have all the watches, but we have all the time." To understand what happened after 2004, it will be important to interrupt the narrative and turn to the study of the nature of 21st-century insurgency.

6. Insurgency: Theory and Practice

An *insurgency* "is an organized movement aimed at the overthrow of a constituted government through the use of subversion or armed conflict."[1] Insurgency—sometimes called guerrilla warfare—presents unique problems for the host government:

Analogically, the guerrilla fights the war of the flea, and his military enemy suffers the dog's disadvantages: too much to defend; too small, ubiquitous, and agile an enemy to come to grips with. If the war continues long enough—this is the theory—the dog succumbs to exhaustion and anemia without ever having found anything on which to close his jaws or to rake with his claws.[2]

Insurgencies, whether classical or contemporary, tend to be protracted conflicts where the insurgents bet their assets, support, and will against a weak government's staying power, its generally superior resources, and outside support. Rather than force-on-force conventional operations, where combatants fight to destroy one another, capture terrain, or break alliances, opponents in insurgencies fight for the support—some would say control—of the populace. And contrary to Taber's prediction, the dogs (counterinsurgents) often conquer or outlast the fleas (guerrillas).

The most prominent theorist of insurgency was Mao Zedong. His writings were central to his party's securing victory in mainland China and inspired many other movements, especially the Vietnamese, who took his theory and adapted it to a more modern age and a different milieu. Other movements were inspired by Mao but adopted their own techniques. In Maoist guerrilla warfare, the insurgents move through three stages though not always in a consistent, uniform, or coordinated fashion: an agitation-propaganda phase, where they would establish bases and prepare the battlefield and the population for the struggle; a defensive phase where they would begin guerrilla warfare operations against the government and terrorism against the resistant population; and finally an offensive phase, where the increasingly powerful guerrilla bands—grown strong on their successes in phase 2—could fight as conventional forces, confronting government forces in direct combat.[3]

Insurgents today often bypass Mao's first phase and let armed conflict speak for itself, filling in around the edges with subversion, terrorism, dispute resolution, and, at times, humanitarian aid to enhance the appeal of their arms. Modern insurgencies take various forms and can be divided according to ends, ways, and means.[4] In Afghanistan, the Taliban can be characterized as a reactionary-traditionalist insurgency. It wants to turn the clock back to a form of government that would fit the year 800. It is fighting to regain political power, oust the foreign occupiers, and restore its version of sharia law. Al Qaeda, for its part, seeks to regain or at least maintain a sanctuary in a friendly country, while bleeding the United States and its allies. Afghanistan was the initial state in the development of a multiregional caliphate. The al Qaeda position in Afghanistan was far more secure and productive than its underground existence today in Pakistan.

Throughout their operations, guerrillas emphasize deception and survivability. In Mao's terms, they attack where the government is weak; where the enemy is strong, they refuse battle; where it is temporarily weak, the guerrillas harass, always ready to run away, a tactic that has to be a specialty of insurgents if they are to survive. Most theorists agree with the old saw popularized by David Galula. A revolutionary war—his umbrella term for insurgency and counterinsurgency—"is 20 percent military action and 80 percent political."[5] For the government's forces to win, in his words, they must isolate the insurgents from the people, and "that isolation [must] not [be] enforced upon the population but maintained by and with the population."[6]

There are two basic approaches to counterinsurgency (COIN): counterguerrilla, which emphasizes the destruction of the guerrilla formations and cadres while downplaying nation-building and efforts to gain popular support; and population-centric, which focuses on protection of the population and winning its support. The latter is the U.S. style of COIN. David Galula is its patron saint, and its current bible is Marine Corps and Army Field Manual (FM) 3–24, *Counterinsurgency*.

Most population-centric counterinsurgency theorists believe that the population's perception of the host government's legitimacy—its right to rule—is essential to victory even if it is hard to define and varies from culture to culture.[7] The troubled host government must cultivate and reinforce its legitimacy as the insurgents fight to destroy it, ultimately overthrowing the government to thereby win the victory. Being able to provide security contributes, in great measure, to the perception of legitimacy. Other indicators are regularized leader selection, high levels of political participation, "a culturally acceptable level of corruption," "a culturally acceptable level and rate" of development, and "a high level of regime acceptance by major social institutions."[8]

In a population-centric COIN operation, a counterinsurgent nation and its coalition partners will likely favor a "whole-of-government" or even a "whole-of-society" approach to defeating the insurgency. This unified effort is difficult to achieve. At the same time, military personnel will find themselves enmeshed in military and nonmilitary lines of operation: combat operations and civil security, developing host-nation security forces, delivering essential services, governance, economic development, and information operations.[9] Diplomats, aid workers, international organizations, and NGOs will have close and often uncomfortable working relationships with military forces in insurgencies. The aid organizations' discomfort will be magnified by the fact that aid workers and international organizations are soft targets for insurgents eager to show the government's impotence.

The current U.S. approach to COIN has often incorrectly been portrayed as primarily nonkinetic efforts to "win hearts and minds." While the doctrine is essentially population centric, it allows for offensive, defensive, and stability operations in varying degrees, depending on objectives and local circumstances. For example, in an initial phase where the counterinsurgents are fighting to clear areas of insurgents, offensive operations might dominate the mixture. During the "hold" phase, defense and stability operations might dominate. In the "build" and "transition" phases, stability operations—humanitarian activities, reconstruction, and police and army training—might dominate the counterinsurgent's agenda.[10] Both the surge operations in Iraq and Afghanistan have been marked by controlled, offensive kinetic operations.

Other theories stress the importance of counterguerrilla operations and deemphasize nonmilitary lines of operation. A recent book by Mark Moyar of the Marine Corps University suggests a third approach: that counterinsurgency is "'leader-centric' warfare . . . in which the elite with superiority in certain leadership attributes usually wins. The better elite gains the assistance of more people and uses them to subdue or destroy its enemy's elite and its supporters."[11] No one can downplay the importance of creative and dedicated leadership in any form of warfare, but this approach to counterinsurgency is security-focused and, at the limit, is more akin to counterguerrilla operations than population-centric counterinsurgency.[12] All that said, an insurgency can end in a victory of arms even if counterguerrilla operations are the focal point and the support of the people appears a lesser concern. A strong, strategically focused counterinsurgency effort, coupled with progress in governance, rule of law, and basic economic development, can cover all of the approaches to dealing with insurgency.

Twenty-first-century insurgencies are affected by globalization, the Internet, and the explosion of global media. They are often referred to as "fourth generation warfare," or evolved insurgencies.[13] Information and communication today are paramount. Religion can play the role of ideology, and clerics the role of a party leadership. Sadly, terrorism against the resistant population has always been a constant. Information operations, where the creation or reinforcement of a message or theme is the objective, are an important part of evolved 21st-century insurgencies. In Afghanistan, Lieutenant General Dave Barno, the commander of U.S. forces in Afghanistan from 2003 to 2005, has often noted that the Taliban design the message and then plan the operation around its creation, while the U.S. tends to see information operations as an after action issue.[14] In Afghanistan, the word gets out quickly, aided now by nationwide cell phone service and many radio stations. Civilian casualties and collateral damage are favorite enemy propaganda themes, even though the Taliban was responsible for over 70 percent of civilian casualties in 2010.

Among the most pernicious messages used by al Qaeda and the Taliban is that the United States and its coalition partners are occupying forces who are in Afghanistan to make war on Islam or Afghan culture. In reality, the contest is between Muslims over what their faith is and will be, and whether they will be governed by a backward-looking authoritarian theocracy or a decent civil government. The Taliban wants a radical Islamic state with recourse to terrorism. Most Afghans oppose that radical way, especially its emphasis on indiscriminate killing and promotion of suicidal acts. Many moderate Afghans, however, are outside the protection of the government and its international partners. They may have to sit on the fence and not resist the Taliban.

In addition to the hardcore Taliban, many of whom have never known anything but war, there are what David Kilcullen, an influential advisor to the U.S. Government on COIN issues, calls "accidental guerrillas" who fight because foreign forces are there, or because there is adventure in combat.[15] Allied with the accidental guerrillas are what one might call economic guerrillas, the "five (some say ten) dollar-a-day" Taliban who fight for money. There may be as many motives behind the Taliban insurgency as there are Taliban fighters. Some follow their leaders and are fellow travelers of the radicals in al Qaeda. Many more local Taliban have more prosaic motives.

Drugs, smuggling, kidnapping, and extortion go hand-in-hand with evolved insurgency in Afghanistan. Opium is at the root of these problems. The cultivation of the opium poppy has deep roots in the southern part of the country, the poppies themselves are hardy and drought resistant, and although the farmers are exploited by the drug lords, the farmer's profit per acre from poppy exceeds nearly all other cash crops. Moreover, the farmers are heavily in debt to the drug lords and local money lenders. These debts are matters of honor. The poppy farmer will defend his crops because his deepest interests are in the success of his harvest. Eradication programs can alienate the poppy growing (or reliant) population.

Drug traffic in Afghanistan is among the main sources of funding for the Taliban, which is sometimes involved directly with drug production, but otherwise taxes it or protects it for large fees and payoffs to the leadership in Pakistan. "Charity," mainly from people in the Persian Gulf region, is another source of Taliban funding, and some intelligence analysts believe it is more lucrative than the drug trade.[16] Some experts believe that, through taxation and other payments in kind, the Taliban as a whole may net as much as a half billion dollars a year from the drug trade, which also exerts a corrupting influence on host governments.[17]

Measuring progress in an insurgency is as important as it is tricky. Without metrics, the counterinsurgent will neither learn nor adapt. Input metrics are readily available but are not very useful. Output or achievement measures need to be developed and then tailored for the environment and the state of the operation. As always, staffs will have to fight for information and build their systems on small unit reporting. For their role, unit commanders have to be dedicated to collecting intelligence and feeding the unit metric systems. The reader can find guides to COIN metrics in FM 3–24 or a recent book by Kilcullen.[18]

Without access to detailed metrics can an understanding of counterinsurgency theory help to assess where we are in Afghanistan? Yes, but only generally. Galula suggests that there are four key conditions for a successful insurgency: a sound and lasting cause based on a serious problem; police and administrative weakness in government; a supportive geographical environment; and outside aid to the insurgency. These criteria tell us that we are in for a stressful contest in Afghanistan, but victory is not guaranteed for either side.[19]

The Taliban's primary cause is religion and the need to gain political power by ousting foreign powers and their Afghan "puppet" allies. This cause, on the one hand, creates some fervor, but on the other hand, it brings bad memories to the people. The Taliban's version of Islam rubs many Afghans the wrong way. The inadequacies of Taliban cadres and the disastrous 5 years of Taliban rule are well remembered by all. The Taliban's inhumane treatment of Afghans—especially non-Pashtuns—will work against it in the long run.

The weakness and corruption of the government and the limitations of its coalition partners reinforce the Taliban's efforts and give credence to its cause. The Taliban's ability to use its version of sharia law and its ubiquitous mullahs to settle disputes is a further help. The government's inability to control narcotics not only mocks its power and authority, but it pays the Taliban handsomely and fuels corruption throughout the country. Afghanistan has flooded Western Europe and Russia with opiates. There are growing urban drug problems in Afghan cities, Iran, and Pakistan. There are even drug abuse problems within the Afghan National Security Forces (ANSF). These weaknesses in the Karzai regime and the ANSF can be redressed. The current surge of NATO forces and their efforts to build capacity and combat corruption may help in that regard. In 2011, the allies and the Afghans are close to achieving the troop to population ratio recommended by FM 3–24—20 counterinsurgents for every 1,000 people—and outnumber the Taliban by more than 10 to 1.[20] Better security nationwide is in sight.

At the same time, the geographic environment—especially in southern and eastern Afghanistan and the adjacent areas of Pakistan—is favorable to an insurgency. Road building, local security forces, and creative security assistance can work against this terrain advantage. Outside help from elements in Pakistan, which serves as a secure sanctuary with ample material resources, is adequate for the insurgency today. Pakistan reportedly has begun to work with Taliban groups to make peace with Afghanistan, which appears increasingly in its interest due to the growth of radical behavior in the anti-Islamabad Pakistani Taliban. Sadly, Pakistan maintains a relationship with other radical groups, such as the Lashkar-i-Taiba, a violent, Pakistan-based international terrorist group. So far, outside aid to the legitimate Afghan government can balance aid and the value of sanctuary to the Afghan Taliban. A guerrilla, however, needs far less funding than a legitimate government.

Breaking down overseas support for the Taliban, disrupting their sanctuaries, effective counternarcotics programs, well-selected drone strikes, and working with Pakistan to put pressure on its "guests" should be the order of the day. Building Afghan security and governmental capacity might well be the most important policy focus in this counterinsurgency. But all of this takes the reader ahead of the narrative. To see what must be done, one must first analyze the record from 2002 to the present.

7. The Second War Against the Taliban and the Struggle to Rebuild Afghanistan

Allied commanders and diplomats who arrived in Afghanistan in January 2002 were astounded at the devastation brought about by over two decades of war. The economy and society also suffered mightily from 5 years of Taliban mismanagement and authoritarian rule, further complicated by years of drought. The country they found was only 30 percent literate, and 80 percent of its schools had been destroyed in various wars. The Taliban severely restricted female education and did little for that of males. Twenty-five percent of all Afghan children died before the age of five. Only 9 percent of the population had access to health care. The professional and blue collar work forces had virtually disappeared.[1] The former Afghan finance minister and noted scholar Ashraf Ghani and Clare Lockhart, a British development expert, wrote that:

> Between 1978, when the Communist coup took place, and November 2001, when the Taliban were overthrown, Afghanistan (according to a World Bank estimate) lost $240 billion in ruined infrastructure and vanished opportunities. While the rest of the world was shrinking in terms of spatial and temporal coordination, the travel time between Kabul and every single province in the country significantly increased. Whereas it used to take a minimum of three hours to reach the city of Jalalabad in eastern Afghanistan and six hours to get to the city of Kandahar in the south, in 2002 the roads were so bad that it took fourteen hours to reach Jalalabad and nearly twenty-four hours to get to Kandahar. Millions of Afghan children grew up illiterate in refugee camps,

where they learned that the gun rather than the ballot was the key instrument for the acquisition of power and influence.[2]

Starting from the rock bottom in nearly every category, the government of Afghanistan and its coalition partners had a relatively easy time from 2002 to 2004. Progress was made in security, stabilization, and economic reconstruction. From 2003 to 2005, the U.S. leadership team, led by Ambassador Khalilzad and General Barno, focused on teamwork and elementary organization for counterinsurgency operations, albeit with very small forces. LTG Barno unified the field commands and divided the country into regional areas of responsibility where one colonel or general officer would command all maneuver units and PRTs.

Pursuant to the U.S. initiative and a series of NATO decisions, ISAF's mandate was increasingly enlarged until it took over all of the regions of Afghanistan. In the fall of 2004, NATO and ISAF took charge of the regional command in the north. In the spring of 2006, they took over the west. That summer, ISAF control moved into the south, and in the fall it took over fighting and peacekeeping in the east, marking ISAF command over coalition forces in the entire country. By 2006, most U.S. forces were put under the new, enlarged, and empowered ISAF. While NATO's action brought the Alliance on line in Afghanistan, it also magnified the issue of national "caveats" identified by capitals to limit the activities of their forces. Many NATO nations do not allow their forces to engage in offensive combat operations. The United States, Canada, the United Kingdom, Denmark, the Netherlands, and a few others did most of the fighting and combat advising.[3]

From 2003 to 2005, the relationship between Ambassador Khalilzad and President Karzai was very close and productive. The government of

Afghanistan, with much help from the international community, conducted nationwide loya jirgas (2002, 2003), passed a modern constitution modeled on the 1964 Afghanistan constitution, and held fair presidential and parliamentary elections in 2004 and 2005, respectively.[4] Sadly, the new constitution was highly centralized and gave the president much of the power that the king held in the constitutional monarchy. While the Kabul government was weak, it was responsible for policy and all significant personnel appointments. Warlords still played major roles, but with Japanese funding and UN leadership, the central government confiscated and cantoned all heavy weapons. This process was called disarmament, demobilization, and reintegration. By mid-2004, major fighting between warlords with heavy weapons was no longer an important issue.

Afghanistan attracted a fair amount of international aid, but far less than the Balkan nations did after their conflicts in the 1990s. U.S. security and economic assistance from 2002 to 2004 was a modest $4.4 billion, but nearly two-thirds of it went to economic assistance, leaving slightly more than a third for security assistance. From 2002 to 2004, the average yearly U.S. security and economic assistance, per capita, was only $52 per Afghan.[5] RAND experts contrasted that with nearly $1,400 per capita for Bosnia and over $800 in Kosovo in their first 2 years.[6] The Bush administration had hoped that the United Nations and the IFIs would lead reconstruction and stabilization. It learned that the international actors would only follow in areas where the United States led. Initiatives by so-called lead nations generally proved disappointing. The lack of progress in the development of the police, counternarcotics, and promotion of the rule of law was particularly noteworthy.

On the security front, the build-up of the Afghan National Army was slow but deliberate. The ANA was small but successful and popular among the people. Police development in the first few years was very slow and unproductive, except in the German-sponsored education of commissioned officers. By 2008, 70 percent of U.S. funds went to security assistance or counternarcotics. The figures in the table on page 69 do not include America's expenditures on its own forces, which dwarfed funding for security and economic assistance to Afghanistan.

In the early years, under the guidance of Finance Minister Ashraf Ghani, the Afghan government swapped out the several currencies in use across the country, established a single stable currency, negotiated international contracts for a nationwide cellular phone service, and began economic reconstruction. With the help of the international community, there was rapid reconstruction in health care and education. The United States and international financial institutions began to rebuild the Ring Road, furthering travel and commerce. Access to medical care was extended from 9 percent of the population under the Taliban to 85 percent by 2010.[7] Spurred by foreign aid, rapid legal economic growth began and has continued, but it exists alongside a booming illegal economy marked by bribery, smuggling, and narcotics trafficking.

To make up for inherent weakness in the Afghan government, various countries, following the U.S. lead, set up Provincial Reconstruction Teams. The generic purposes of the PRTs were to further security, promote reconstruction, facilitate cooperation with NGOs and IOs in the area, and help the local authorities in governance and other issues. These small interagency elements were initially established in a third of the provinces but now can be found nearly nationwide. These 26 teams—half led by U.S. allies—today play a key role in reconstruction and development. PRTs consist of a headquarters, a security element, and civil affairs teams, as well as diplomats, aid and assistance experts, and, where possible, agricultural teams. Also, without a nationwide peacekeeping force, these teams were often the only way diplomats and government aid professionals could get out to the countryside. From 2002 to 2009, the U.S.-hosted PRTs have been instrumental in disbursing nearly $2.7 billion in Commander's Emergency Response Program funds and other PRT-designated moneys.[8]

PRTs have been a positive development. They have, however, exacerbated civil-military tensions within the U.S. Government and led to recurring problems with international financial institutions and NGOs, which are still not used to having military forces in the "humanitarian space." Some donors found the PRTs a convenient excuse to ignore the need to build Afghan government capacity. While many observers objected to the military flavor of the teams, the need for strong security elements dictated that role. Regional commanders after 2004 controlled maneuver forces and PRTs in their region.[9] "In 2009, the U.S. Ambassador put civilian leadership at the brigade and Regional Command levels, creating a civilian hierarchical structure that mirrors the military [chain of command]."[10] The concept of PRTs was later exported to Iraq, where they were put under State Department management. There, some PRTs were geographic and others were embedded with troop units. Post-2009, the U.S. Government has also used District Support Teams in Afghanistan, with representatives from State, the U.S. Agency for International Development (USAID), and the Department of Agriculture. These teams go with deployed military units or other security elements to hot spots to work directly with Afghan government representatives. There were 19 of these teams in Regional Command East (RC–E) alone. In a similar vein, the U.S. National Guard fielded nine Agribusiness

U.S. Aid to Afghanistan

(All accounts, by fiscal year, in $US millions, including supplementals)

	2002–2004	2005–2006	2007–2008	Percent 2002–2004	Percent 2005–2006	Percent 2007–2008
Security	1,484	4,296	10,194	34	51	64
ANA	1,166	2,369	6,650	26	28	42
ANP	184	1,841	3,487	4	22	22
Other Security	134	86	57	3	1	0
Counternarcotics	169	880	947	4	10	6
Interdiction	80	475	574	2	6	4
Eradication	89	395	360	2	5	2
Other CN	0	10	13	0	0	0
Dev/Hum	2,772	3,247	4,808	63	39	30
Dem/Gov	425	303	655	10	4	4
Reconstruction	1,275	1,946	2,636	29	23	17
Alt Livelihood	0	315	409	0	4	3
Rule of Law	44	51	191	1	1	1
Hum/Other	1,028	632	917	23	8	6
Total	4,425	8,423	15,949	100	100	100

Source: U.S. Embassy Kabul, 2009, provided by Ambassador William Wood.

69

Development Teams with military and state university agronomists to help Afghan agriculture and animal husbandry enter the 21st century.

In terms of reconstruction and development, the coalition, reinforced by the United Nations and international financial institutions, did yeoman's work and markedly improved Afghanistan's lot. Through the end of fiscal year (FY) 2009, nearly $40 billion in U.S. foreign and security assistance were pledged or delivered. Other nations and international financial institutions delivered at least $14 billion in economic assistance through FY08. There is no reliable source for what U.S. allies spend on security assistance.[11] This huge sum for economic and security assistance, however, comes to only a few hundred dollars per Afghan per year.

Progress in health care, road building, and some areas of agriculture has been excellent. A RAND study, citing NATO statistics, noted that the military and development wings of allied nations had built or repaired tens of thousands of kilometers of roads.[12] So while it is fair to note that the areas under the most Taliban pressure received the least aid, there were significant accomplishments generally. Five million refugees have returned, school enrollment has increased sixfold from Taliban days, and 35 percent of the students are female. For its part, the Taliban had burned or bombed over 1,000 schools in the 2007–2009 period. USAID alone, to the end of 2008, spent over $7 billion helping the Afghan people. It had the following accomplishments:

+ 715 km of the Kabul to Kandahar to Herat Highway reconstructed

+ 1,700 km of paved and 1,100 km of gravel roads completed

+ 670 clinics or health facilities constructed or refurbished

- ✦ 10,600 health workers trained including doctors, midwives, and nurses
- ✦ $6 million of pharmaceuticals distributed
- ✦ 670 schools constructed or refurbished
- ✦ 60 million textbooks printed and distributed nationwide in Dari and Pashto
- ✦ 65,000 teachers trained in modern teaching methods
- ✦ 494,000 hectares of land received improved irrigation
- ✦ 28,118 loans made to small businesses, 75 percent to women
- ✦ 28 million livestock vaccinated/treated
- ✦ over 500 PRT quick impact projects completed.[13]

In all, the coalition did well in the first few years, but not well enough. Despite significant economic gains, poverty remained widespread and the insurgents did their best to disrupt the progress and interfere with aid workers. The level of international aid was not enough to stem the tide of an insurgency designed in part to frustrate it. Afghanistan had encountered the eternal truism of insurgency that Galula noted in the 1960s: Order is the government's goal; disorder is the insurgent's goal.

Moreover, disorder—the normal state of nature—is cheap to create and very costly to prevent. The insurgent blows up a bridge, so every bridge has to be guarded; he throws a grenade into a movie theater, so every person entering a public place has to be searched. . . . Because the counterinsurgent cannot escape the responsibility for maintaining order, the ratio of expenses between

*him and the insurgent is high. It may be ten or twenty to one,
or higher.*[14]

What Went Wrong in Afghanistan?

From 2002 to 2005, the Taliban rebuilt its cadres with drug money, "charity" from donors in the Gulf states, and help from al Qaeda. Their sanctuaries in Pakistan enabled them to rearm, refit, and retrain. By 2005, the Quetta Shura Taliban, led by Mullah Omar; the Hezb-i-Islami Gulbuddin, led by Gulbuddin Hekmatyar; and the Haqqani Network, lead by Jalaluddin Haqqani and his son, Sirajuddin, were all working together to subvert the Karzai regime and wear down the coalition. All three groups swear at least nominal allegiance to Mullah Omar and coordinate major plans, but they are distinct operational entities with their own territories of interest in Afghanistan as well as fundraising mechanisms. Mullah Omar is also revered by the Pakistani Taliban, who have opposed Pakistan's government after 2006. In 2005, the Afghan government's lack of capacity and the allies' "light footprint" allowed many districts and a few provinces to fall under the quiet "shadow" control of the Taliban. In fact, some provinces, such as poppy-rich Helmand, had very little government or coalition presence before 2006.

In 2005, the Taliban began a nationwide offensive to spread its influence. From 2004 to 2009, there was a ninefold increase in security incidents nationwide, and a fortyfold increase in suicide bombing. Conflict spread to most of the 34 provinces, but 71 percent of the security incidents in 2010 took place in only 10 percent of the nearly 400 districts nationwide.[15] The war in Afghanistan today is still primarily a war over control of Pashtun areas in the eastern and southern portion of the country, but Taliban subversion and terrorism have become important factors in many provinces. Efforts to combat narcotics growth and production generally failed or met with only temporary success. Corruption inside Afghanistan as well as Taliban revenue increased accordingly.

With lessons learned through al Qaeda in Iraq, the use of Improvised Explosive Devices (IEDs) became the tactic of choice of the Taliban. IED strikes went from 300 in 2004 to more than 4,000 in 2009. By the summer of 2010, more than half of all U.S. fatalities in Afghanistan were coming from IEDs.[16] Suicide bombers, almost unknown before 2004, became commonplace.

By 2009, there were Taliban shadow governments in nearly all provinces, although many had little real influence and not all of them lived in the designated provinces.[17] Even in areas dominated by the government or government-friendly tribes, Taliban subversion or terror tactics have become potent facts of life.

Beginning in 2005, the Taliban added more sophisticated information operations and local subversion to their standard terrorist tactics. The "night letters" of the Soviet-Afghan war era—a way to warn or intimidate the population—made a comeback. Among examples published by ISAF in August 2010, the first threatens students, teachers, and parents:

Islamic Emirate of Afghanistan, Maulawi Jalaludeen Haqani: This warning goes to all students, teachers, and personnel of Mohammad Sedeque Rohi High School. This high school has violated Mujahidin's established standards for education. Since the high school has taken a negative stand against Mujahidin, it is Mujahidin's final resolution to burn the high school to the ground or destroy it with a suicide attack, should any negative propaganda or information regarding Mujahidin be discussed in the future at the school.

The next night letter, written over a drawing of a large knife, warns those who work for Americans:

Afghanistan Islamic Emirate, Kandahar province: We Mujahi-din received information that you and your son are working for Americans. You cannot hide from Mujahidin, we will find you. If you and your son do not stop working for Americans then we will cut you and your son's heads with the knife that you see in this letter. Anybody who is working with the American will be punished with the knife that you see in this letter.

The next letter threatens children for fraternizing with coalition soldiers:

Attention to all dear brothers: If the infidels come to your villages or to your mosques, please stop your youngsters from working for them and don't let them walk with the infidels. If anybody in your family is killed by a mine or anything else, then you will be the one responsible, not us.[18]

Sadly, in addition to subversion, terror tactics remained standard operating procedure for the Taliban. In October 2008, for example, "the Taliban stopped a bus in the town of Maiwand, forcibly removed 50 passengers, and beheaded 30 of them."[19] A UN study in 2010 noted that:

The human cost of the armed conflict in Afghanistan is escalating in 2010. In the first six months of the year civilian casualties — including deaths and injuries of civilians — increased by 31 per cent over the same period in 2009. Three quarters of all civilian

casualties were linked to Anti-Government Elements (AGEs), an
increase of 53 per cent from 2009. At the same time, civilian
casualties attributed to Pro-Government Forces (PGF) decreased
by 30 per cent compared to the first half of 2009.[20]

While the population appreciates coalition restraint, the terror tactics of the Taliban have kept many Pashtuns on the fence.

Explaining the Lack of Progress

How did the war in Afghanistan degenerate from a quiet front in the war on terrorism to a hyperactive one? First, in the early years, there was little progress in building Afghan capacity for governance, security, or economic development. There was so little Afghan government and administrative capacity that much economic and security assistance bypassed the central government. Nations and international organizations found it more convenient to work through NGOs and contractors. In later years, these habits continued and corruption among Afghan government officials increased. Over the years, the government in turn lost key ministers such as Ashraf Ghani (finance), Abdullah Abdullah (foreign affairs), and Ali Jalali, an early minister of the interior. After the departure of Ambassador Khalilzad in 2005, Karzai lost his closest confidant on the American side. Subsequent Ambassadors—Ronald Neumann, William Wood, and Karl Eikenberry—did fine work but did not have the close relationship that existed between Karzai and Khalilzad.

The coalition widened, and NATO, which served as the overseer of the ISAF-assigned forces since 2003, took over the south and later the east in 2006.[21] Some Afghans and Pakistanis saw these efforts as a sign of a weakening American commitment to the long war, despite the fact that over time, more and more U.S. forces were assigned to ISAF, which came to be commanded by an American general.

There was also much government corruption, often tied to police operations or the drug trade. Karzai took the lead in dealing with the so-called warlords, the regional strongmen. Many of them ended up in the government. Others continued their viral existence in the provinces, often using their local power and cunning to take money from reconstruction projects and even U.S. security contracts. Money laundering through Kabul International Airport became well developed. Pallets of convertible currencies were moved to the United Arab Emirates by individuals, corporations, and Afghan government officials.[22] President Karzai's brothers and immediate subordinates have also become the subject of corruption investigations.

Second, coalition arms, aid, trainers, and advisors ended up being too little, too slow, and too inefficient. The U.S. "light footprint" strategy in 2002–2004 was inadequate to the task and to the capacity of the threat. U.S. and allied combat troops fared well, but the coalition was unsuccessful in building the capacity of the Afghan security forces, especially the police. Responsibility for police training bounced from Germany to the State Department to the U.S. Department of Defense. In early 2010, parts of that effort were still in transition, and Army and police trainer/ advisors remained in short supply. Coalition operations in Afghanistan have also become a nightmare of "contractorization," with more Western-sponsored contractors—many armed—than soldiers in country. This in part reflects the limitations of relatively small volunteer forces and the ravages of protracted conflict. The police were an especially weak link in the security chain, and the Taliban has made attacking the ANP a priority. From 2007 to 2009, Afghan security personnel killed in action (3,046) outnumbered U.S. and allied dead (nearly 800) by more than 3 to 1.[23] More than two out of three of the Afghan personnel killed were police.

In all, from 2004 to 2009, there were insufficient coalition forces or Afghan National Security Forces to "clear, hold, and build," and nowhere near enough capacity to "transfer" responsibility to Afghan forces. The Taliban had a wide pool of unemployed tribesmen and former militia fighters to recruit from, as well as greater latitude in picking targets. By 2009, the war of the flea spread from its home base in the Pashtun areas in the south and east to the entire nation.

In the early years, coalition offensive military efforts often resembled the game of "Whack-a-mole," where a sweep would go after the Taliban, who would go into hiding until the coalition forces left. Taliban penetration of many areas deepened. Subversion, terrorism, and night letters from the local Taliban ruled many apparently safe districts by night. In areas with scant Pashtun populations, the Taliban also used motorcycle squads and IEDs for controlling the population. Since 2006, Taliban judges have administered sharia-based judgments, trumping Karzai's slow and sometimes corrupt civil courts. The Afghan people have had little love for the Taliban, but insecurity has made them hesitant to act against them.

It is not true that initial U.S. operations in Iraq (2003–2004) stripped Afghanistan of what it needed to fight the Taliban. But 2004 was the last "good" year for Afghan security. While some Intelligence, Surveillance, and Reconnaissance assets and Special Forces units had been removed from Afghanistan, most of the assets needed to continue the operation were wisely "fenced" by Pentagon and USCENTCOM planners before the invasion of Iraq.[24] It is fair to say, however, that post-2005, as the situation in Afghanistan began to decline, the greater scope and intensity of problems in Iraq prevented reinforcements or additional funds from being sent to Afghanistan. Another policy fault plagued U.S. war efforts: while U.S. fortunes declined in two wars, U.S. Department of Defense leadership refused to expand the end strength of the U.S. Armed Forces until 2006. For a short time, the Pentagon slightly reduced U.S. troops in Afghanistan when NATO took over command and control of the mission that year.

One example of insufficient support to our efforts from Washington could be classified as typical. Noting the increase in enemy activity and the paucity of foreign assistance programs, Ambassador Ronald E. Neumann in October 2005 requested an additional $601 million for roads, power, agriculture, counternarcotics, and PRT support. The State Department reduced the figure to $400 million, but in the end, not including debt relief, national decisionmakers disallowed all but $32 million of the $601 million the Embassy requested. Neumann concluded, "I believed then and suspect now that the decision was driven by the desire to avoid too large a budget; Iraq and hurricane relief won and we lost." Secretary Rice could not do anything about it. As the Taliban offensive intensified, no other nation or institution made up for the shortfall. Human and fiscal reinforcement came in 2007, but some felt that it was too little too late.[25]

The regional powers—Saudi Arabia, Pakistan, Iran, India, Russia, and China—did little to help. Each had its own interests and timetables. Iran and Pakistan were part of the problem, and the other four were unable to further a solution. Pakistan was wary of American staying power and hedged its bets, allowing the Afghan Taliban to operate from its territory with minimal interference. Iran was no friend of the Taliban, and it worked (often with bags of cash) to further its interests with authorities in Kabul and in the western part of Afghanistan in an effort to improve trade and border control. Tehran, however, has also erratically aided the Taliban to ensure an American quagmire, if not outright defeat. India gave over $1 billion in aid and was helpful on the commercial end. It worked hard to earn contracts in Afghanistan and forged a logistical alliance with Iran to work around Pakistan's geographic advantages. Saudi Arabia tried to use its good offices to end the war but was frustrated by the Afghan Taliban's refusal to break relations with al Qaeda, a sworn enemy of the Kingdom of Saudi Arabia. Russia and China exploited commercial contacts, and Russia slowly began to improve counternarcotics cooperation with the coalition. In later years, Russia participated with other regional nations in forming a northern logistics route. China is poised today to help Afghanistan develop its mineral deposits. More is said on the regional powers in the final chapter.

In all, by 2009, the regional powers were not the primary cause of the war in Afghanistan, but their policies have not worked toward a solution. Pakistan is particularly noteworthy. While the U.S. policy—correct in my view—has been one of patient engagement to wean Islamabad from its dysfunctional ways, analysts from other countries could be openly bitter. One Canadian historian who served in Afghanistan wrote that Pakistan was behind the external support to the insurgents in southern Afghanistan: "To pretend that Pakistan is anything but a failed state equipped with nuclear weapons, and a country with a 50-year history of exporting low-intensity warfare as a strategy, ignores the 800-pound gorilla in the room."[26]

By the end of the Bush administration, security was down, as was Afghan optimism about the future. Afghan confidence in the United States and its allies was halved in 2008. Many Afghans believed the Taliban had grown stronger every year since 2005, and incentives for fence-sitting increased along with fear and disgust at government corruption. Polls in Afghanistan rebounded in 2009 with a new U.S. administration and the prospect for elections in Afghanistan. Karzai's popularity plummeted in the West after widespread fraud in the 2010 presidential elections. The Obama administration clearly needed a new strategy.[27]

Events in Afghanistan were trying, but the nearly desperate situation in Iraq up to mid-2007 kept U.S. leaders from focusing on them. It was not until the obvious success of the surge in Iraq that U.S. decisionmakers—late in the Bush administration—were able to turn their attention to the increasingly dire situation in Afghanistan. With the advent of the Obama administration and improvements in Iraq, Afghanistan became the top priority in the war on terrorism. By the summer of 2010, there were more than two U.S. Soldiers in Afghanistan for every one in Iraq. In fall 2010, there were nearly as many non-Afghan allied soldiers in the country (40,000) as there were American Soldiers still in Iraq. The policy that brought that about was also called the surge, despite some significant differences with its sibling in Iraq.

8. The Surge

The United States decided to surge in Afghanistan to reinforce its commitment with military and civilian assets as well as more resources, but it took nearly a year to bring it to fruition.[1] The foundation of the surge was laid by President George W. Bush in 2008, but the construction was completed under President Obama in 2009 and 2010. Studies on our strategy in Afghanistan began in the last year of the Bush administration. The most critical study of all was reportedly conducted under the auspices of the Bush NSC staff.[2] There was a preliminary decision to recommend an increase in forces to President Bush, but it was delayed to give the new team a chance to study the situation and make its own recommendations. Early on, President Obama and his team conducted studies that incorporated the work of the previous administration. Bruce Reidel of RAND, a former CIA executive, supervised the efforts, which were facilitated by the continued presence on the NSC staff of Lieutenant General Doug Lute, USA, who managed the war for the previous administration and has remained an essential element of continuity in the U.S. Afghanistan policy.

In March 2009, President Obama made his first set of changes.[3] His March 27 white paper outlined a counterinsurgency program aimed at thwarting al Qaeda, "reversing the Taliban's momentum in Afghanistan," increasing aid to Pakistan and Afghanistan, and forging a more united strategic approach to both countries.[4] Some 21,000 additional U.S. troops were sent to Afghanistan to reinforce the 38,000 American and nearly 30,000 allied forces already there. In 2009, ISAF created an intermediate warfighting headquarters, the ISAF Joint Command, and a new training command, the NATO Training Mission–Afghanistan (NTM–A). In a parallel action, the President replaced the U.S. and ISAF commander, General

David McKiernan, with General Stanley McChrystal, then Director of the Joint Staff and a former commander of special operations elements in both Iraq and Afghanistan. The Secretary of Defense directed McChrystal to conduct an assessment of our current efforts and report back to the White House. His August assessment was leaked to the press. Over the next 3 months, President Obama and his senior advisors conducted a detailed in-house assessment to determine how best to amend U.S. strategy.

President Obama's national security team examined three options. The first came from the field. General McChrystal recommended a beefed-up, population-centric counterinsurgency strategy.[5] He identified two key threats: the vibrant insurgency and a "Crisis of Confidence" in the Karzai regime and the coalition. Among his key recommendations were greater partnering, increasing the size of the Afghan National Security Forces, improving governance, and gaining the initiative from the Taliban. McChrystal also recommended focusing resources on threatened populations, improving counternarcotics efforts, changing the culture of ISAF to make it more population friendly, and adapting restrictive rules of engagement to protect the population more effectively. This last measure quickly showed positive results. ISAF-related civilian casualties were 40 percent of the total in 2008, 25 percent in 2009, and 20 percent to midyear 2010.[6] His initial assessment did not include a request for a troop increase, but he later identified a favored option of 40,000 additional U.S. troops.

Other administration players had different ideas, and they were debated with active participation from President Obama.[7] Some saw a need to focus more directly on al Qaeda, others wanted more emphasis on Pakistan, others wanted a delay because of the weakness of our Afghan allies, and still others saw shifting the priority to building the Afghan National Security Forces (police and military) as the key to victory. Vice

President Joe Biden reportedly advocated a strategy focused on counter-terrorism, with less emphasis on expensive COIN and nation-building. As previously noted, Ambassador Karl Eikenberry, now on his third major assignment in Afghanistan, was concerned with the inefficiency and corruption of the Karzai regime. He famously told Secretary of State Hillary Clinton and President Obama in November 2009 that Karzai "is not an adequate strategic partner."[8] He did not initially concur with U.S. combat troop reinforcements and recommended a shift of the U.S. top priorities to preparing the ANSF to take over security and working more closely with Pakistan.[9]

After 3 months of discussions, President Obama outlined U.S. objectives in a West Point speech. These included defeating al Qaeda, denying it safe haven, preventing the Taliban from taking over Afghanistan, and strengthening the Afghan government:

I am convinced that our security is at stake in Afghanistan and Pakistan. This is the epicenter of violent extremism practiced by al-Qaeda. It is from here that we were attacked on 9/11, and it is from here that new attacks are being plotted as I speak. This is no idle danger, no hypothetical threat. In the last few months alone, we have apprehended extremists within our borders who were sent here from the border region of Afghanistan and Pakistan to commit new acts of terror. And this danger will only grow if the region slides backwards and al-Qaeda can operate with impunity.

We must keep the pressure on al-Qaeda. And to do that, we must increase the stability and capacity of our partners in the region. . . . Our overarching goal remains the same: to disrupt, dismantle and defeat al-Qaeda in Afghanistan and Pakistan and to prevent its capacity to threaten America and our allies in the future.

To meet that goal, we will pursue the following objectives within Afghanistan. We must deny al-Qaeda a safe haven. We must reverse the Taliban's momentum and deny it the ability to overthrow the government. And we must strengthen the capacity of Afghanistan's security forces and government, so that they can take lead responsibility for Afghanistan's future.[10]

To accomplish this, the President directed the reinforcement of an additional 30,000 U.S. troops, with the NATO allies adding nearly 10,000 to that total. Nearly all of those forces were in place by the fall of 2010. To accompany the troop surge, the President ordered a surge of civilian officials, a great increase in foreign assistance, a decisive boost in funding for ANSF, increased aid to Pakistan, and support for Afghan reintegration and reconciliation efforts. By summer 2010, U.S. Government civilians in the country topped 1,050, more than doubling the January 2009 total. Nearly 370 of that number were deployed in the field with regional commands.[11]

By early fall 2010, U.S. forces reached the 100,000 level, and allied forces totaled 41,400. At the same time, the ANA had 144,000 soldiers, formed into 7 corps, each with about 3 brigades per corps. There were also 6 commando battalions and an air force with 40 planes. The Afghan National Police topped 117,000, with over 5,000 of them in Afghan National Civil Order Police units, which receive special training and equipment to perform paramilitary functions. Afghan and ISAF forces were integrated in field operations.[12] In January 2011, a senior U.S.

military officer noted that partnering in the field nationwide was at the one Afghan to one U.S. or allied unit.[13]

At the same time as the increase in personnel and programs, President Obama also made it clear that the United States would not tolerate an "endless war," in his words. He directed that in July 2011 "our troops will begin to come home." He pointed out that the United States must balance all of its commitments and rejected the notion that Afghanistan was another Vietnam. His message attempted to portray a firm national commitment, but not an indeterminate military presence:

> *There are those who acknowledge that we can't leave Afghanistan in its current state, but suggest that we go forward with the troops that we already have. But this would simply maintain a status quo in which we muddle through, and permit a slow deterioration of conditions there. . . . Finally, there are those who oppose identifying a time frame for our transition to Afghan responsibility. Indeed, some call for a more dramatic and open-ended escalation of our war effort—one that would commit us to a nationbuilding project of up to a decade. I reject this course because it sets goals that are beyond what can be achieved at a reasonable cost, and what we need to achieve to secure our interests. . . . It must be clear that Afghans will have to take responsibility for their security, and that America has no interest in fighting an endless war in Afghanistan.[14]*

While this declaration had positive political effects at home, it did create ambiguity and uncertainty among friends and adversaries alike. The administration worked hard to convince all concerned that "7/11" would not signal a rapid withdrawal but rather the beginning of a conditions-based, phased turnover of security to the Afghans. NATO's Lisbon Conference extended this "transition" process until 2014, which is also when President Karzai stated that the ANSF would be able to take over security in each of Afghanistan's 34 provinces. That year also marks the end of his second (and constitutionally final) term.

Improving and deepening relations with Pakistan is an important part of the surge, complementing the increased attention Pakistan received in the final years of the Bush administration. Greater congressional interest resulted in the 5-year, $7.5 billion Kerry-Lugar-Berman economic assistance package in the fall of 2009. Pakistan is larger and richer than Afghanistan and possesses nuclear weapons. It also has a longstanding dispute with India, with whom the United States has begun to forge a strategic relationship. Pakistan's own Taliban—loosely allied with the Afghan Taliban—has increased the inherent instability of that fragile nation, and success in COIN operations in either Pakistan or Afghanistan affects security in the other country. Pakistan's long-term relationship with the Afghan Taliban also makes it a key player in future reconciliation efforts in Afghanistan.

By the summer of 2010, the new U.S. strategy was well under way. Major operations in Helmand and Kandahar did well in the "clear" phase, but struggled in the "hold" and "build" phases. Afghan and coalition governance and police efforts have lagged the military effort. Superb operations by 2d Marine Expeditionary Brigade in Helmand deserve special credit, as do Army efforts in RC–E and allied Special Operations Forces' efforts in taking out Taliban leadership. Village auxiliaries—Afghan Local Police—have also begun to fight under local shura and Ministry of the Interior supervision. With U.S. Special Operations Forces doing the training, coalition authorities plan to expand the local police effort to over 30,000 officers in 100 key districts.[15] Without proper training and supervision, the police effort could backfire, create disorder, or favor the development of warlords.

The greatest and most lasting progress of all was made by the NATO Training Mission–Afghanistan in 2010. With 33 nations participating, the command under U.S. Lieutenant General William Caldwell, USA, which is now funded at over $10 billion per annum, drastically increased and improved training for the Afghan National Army and Police, bringing their combined strength to over 300,000. The command also improved the quality of training and branched out into literacy training for all soldiers and police officers, as well as supporting indigenous industries. The command is still short hundreds of NATO trainers, but it has brought its manning up to 79 percent of the total authorized. The acid test for NTM–A and its partners at ISAF Joint Command who supervise unit partnering in the field will come in the transition period from 2011 to 2014.[16] Thereafter, sustaining a multibillion-dollar-per-year financial commitment for security forces will be a significant challenge.

The civilian surge has helped progress on nonmilitary lines of operation—governance, rule of law, and development—but these areas generally lag behind military-related operations. The Afghan government's ability to receive the transfer of responsibility in cleared areas has been similarly problematic.[17] All criticism aside, however, the rapid build-up of U.S. Government civilians has been remarkable. Their efforts have been guided by the groundbreaking *Integrated Civilian-Military Campaign Plan for Support to Afghanistan*, signed by General McChrystal and Ambassador Eikenberry in August 2009.[18] Today, in addition to Provincial Reconstruction Teams, U.S. Government civilian managers serve at the brigade level and man District Support Teams that give diplomatic, development, and agricultural advice to deployed units and Afghan government officials.

National Guard Agribusiness Development Teams—State civil-military partnerships—give advice to farmers across the country.

One prominent effect of the surge and related activities in Afghanistan and Pakistan has been increased pressure on the enemy.[19] An October 2010 news release by ISAF Joint Command–Afghanistan included the following information:

> *Afghan and coalition security forces spent the month of September continuing to capture and kill key Taliban and Haqqani insurgent leaders, clearing traditional insurgent strong holds and ensuring civilians were able to cast their vote in the Parliamentary election. September marked a total of more than 438 suspected insurgents detained and 114 insurgents killed in security force operations. More importantly, the security force captured or killed more than 105 Haqqani Network and Taliban leaders. These leadership figures include shadow governors, leaders, sub-leaders and weapons facilitators. Afghan and coalition forces completed 194 missions, 88 percent of them without shots fired. The month of September ended on a high note when a precision air strike in Kunar province September 25 killed Abdallah Umar al-Qurayshi, an Al Qaeda senior leader who coordinated the attacks of a group of Arab fighters in Kunar and Nuristan province.[20]*

A subsequent summary of September through November 2010 listed "368 insurgent leaders either killed or captured, 968 lower level fighters killed and 2,477 insurgents captured by coalition forces."[21] Despite these coalition successes, the Taliban has been able to replace its fallen leadership. It remains as of this writing (March 2011) a dangerous, motivated, and adaptive foe.

9. A Current Assessment and Contending Options

After almost 10 years of effort, U.S. and coalition prospects in Afghanistan will be influenced by 5 vectors.[1] U.S. interests remain a guide and provide the first vector. Two American Presidents over a decade have declared that the war is a vital national interest. Nearly a decade after the 9/11 attack, the current administration is still rightfully focused on the defeat or degradation of al Qaeda and its associated movements, one of which is the Afghan Taliban.

The war in Afghanistan has also become the main effort in the U.S. war on terrorism. President Obama in the first 18 months of his administration twice reinforced our Afghanistan contingent. Friendly forces—U.S., allied, and Afghan—in the fall of 2010 included 384,000 military and police personnel, more than 10 times the estimated size of the full-time Taliban fighting force.[2] In his first 20 months in office, according to the New America Foundation, President Obama nearly tripled the total Bush administration 2007–2008 drone strikes against terrorist targets in Pakistan. In 2010, by the end of September, the administration had conducted 50 percent more strikes than it did in all of 2009.[3] In a May 2010 state visit to Washington, President Karzai also received a promise from the Obama administration of a long-term strategic relationship that will cement the U.S.-Afghan partnership beyond the sound of the guns. Vice President Biden reiterated this promise during a visit to Kabul in January 2011.[4]

Second, the costs have been considerable. For the United States, the war has gone on nearly 10 years. For Afghanistan, spring 2011 marks more than three decades of uninterrupted war. By mid-2011, over 1,500 U.S. war dead, 900 fallen allies, and tens of thousands of Afghan dead bear silent witness to the high cost of this protracted conflict.[5] Pakistan has suffered over 30,000 casualties during the war on terrorism.[6] In a 2010 visit to Washington, General Ashfaq Kayani, the Pakistani army chief, reminded his U.S. audiences that in 2009 alone, the Pakistani army suffered 10,000 casualties in its battles against the Pakistani Taliban. Nearly 3,000 members of the Afghan security forces were killed in action from 2007 to 2009. Afghan civilian dead averaged approximately 2,000 per year from 2008 to 2010.[7]

The commitment of NATO nations on both sides of the Atlantic is politically uncertain. In Europe, delicate coalition governments are dealing with significant fiscal problems and low public support for fighting in Afghanistan. American pleas in 2010 for a larger European contribution have been met, but most European and Canadian combat contingents will likely be withdrawn in the next few years. War weariness among all combatants is likely to be a significant change agent as nations count down to 2014, the Lisbon Summit target for the nationwide Afghan takeover of security. Polls in the United States in 2010 showed less than 40 percent of the public supporting the war. U.S. public support was even lower in 2011 polls. At the same time, U.S. voters did not consider the war to be a top-tier electoral issue, as it has been in elections in Canada and the Netherlands.

Popular support for the war has been much lower in Europe than in the United States.[8] While 49 nations are in the NATO-led coalition, burden- and risk-sharing have remained problems. Only Afghanistan, Canada, Denmark, Great Britain, the Netherlands, the United States, and a few other nations pursue full-time offensive combat operations. Washington also outstrips its allies in security- and foreign-assistance spending. Still, the allies added close to 10,000 personnel to their strength in the surge and have suffered over 900 deaths during the war. One recent study found that seven allied nations have taken more fatalities per number of deployed soldiers than the United States. A recent RAND study that measured casualties according to the total end strength in each country's armed forces found 4 nations with more casualties per 100,000 personnel on their rolls than the United States.[9]

U.S. war expenditures in FY10 and FY11 will top $100 billion.[10] This enormous cost—on behalf of a country whose legal gross domestic product (measured in purchasing power parity) is about a fifth of the U.S. budgetary allocation—comes at a time of high unemployment and rampant deficit spending in the United States. In the midterm, budgetary constraints in the United States and Europe will begin to influence how the coalition pursues its objectives in Afghanistan. Between fiscal and strategic concerns, there are growing antiwar issues on both sides of the congressional aisle, with some worried about costs, some worried about corruption, and still others concerned that our expansive strategy is out of touch with our true interests.

Third, the enemy—generally successful from 2005 to 2009—is under great pressure from the coalition on Afghan battlefields. Pakistan is slowly awakening to the danger of harboring violent extremist groups on its territory. Its soldiers have fought a war in Khyber Pakhtunkhwa and South Waziristan to make that point. A massive flood in Pakistan put the war there on hold in the summer and fall of 2010. In Afghanistan, major allied offensives in the Pashtun-dominated south and east of Afghanistan highlighted the coalition's determination. U.S. Treasury experts on al Qaeda funding have stepped up activities against the Taliban's financiers.[11] One of the three major elements of the Afghan Taliban, Gulbuddin Hekmatyar's Hezb-i-Islami faction, has been in contact with the Karzai government. Another part of the Taliban, the Haqqani Network, with close ISI and al Qaeda connections, has reportedly begun exploratory talks, using Pakistan as an intermediary.[12]

This process has a long way to go. In June 2010, Leon Panetta, the head of the CIA, said: "We have seen no evidence that they [that is, the Taliban] are truly interested in reconciliation, where they would surrender their arms, where they would denounce al Qaeda, where they would really try to become part of that society."[13] The Taliban is neither down nor out, but for the first time since the fall of 2001, it is feeling serious pressure from both its enemies and its benefactors. Reconciliation efforts are still in an infant stage.

Fourth, President Karzai's weak government remains the Taliban's best talking point. The government that must win this war seems in some ways less capable than it was in the 2002–2005 period. The police are a hindrance, the bureaucrats are inefficient and corrupt, and the ministries are ineffective. The narcotics industry may be a third the size of the entire legal economy. The effect of narcotics trafficking on Taliban funding and government corruption is profound. Still, the government stands far higher in polls than the Taliban. In the June 2010 Asia Foundation survey, public optimism in Afghanistan was at a 5-year high, as was the public evaluation of government performance.[14] Indeed, the government remains far more popular among Afghans than either the United States or coalition forces.

The level of governmental corruption was evident in the recent presidential election. Only the withdrawal of Karzai's most serious competitor, former foreign minister Abdullah Abdullah, who in all likelihood did not have the votes to win a runoff, enabled the current president to be legitimately called the winner. Public bickering in 2010 had U.S. officials embarrassing Karzai by their public statements, while he bitterly denounced the United States and NATO for acting as occupiers, even once out of frustration suggesting that he might as well join the Taliban. His mid-May 2010 visit to Washington poured oil on these troubled waters, but in the run-up to the September 2010 parliamentary elections, President Karzai appeared to be directly interfering with corruption investigations into his government. The subsequent parliamentary election was problematical but was clearly more legitimate than the previous presidential election. Karzai was reportedly disturbed by the inability to open polls in some conflict areas in the south and east, traditional Pashtun strongholds. By the time the counting was done, there were 15 fewer Pashtun legislators than in the previous parliament.

In the past, friction had been present within the U.S. team—the Embassy, Special Envoy Richard Holbrooke's group, and the military command. It was a factor in the improper and ill-timed complaints by General McChrystal and his staff to a reporter that resulted in the General's ouster from command.[15] By the fall of 2010, however, friction appeared to have abated if press articles were an appropriate gauge. How the untimely death of Ambassador Holbrooke will affect this situation is unknown. While he could be hard to deal with, Holbrooke was a master negotiator and a consummate diplomat. His efforts toward a better peace will be sorely missed.

Despite much economic aid, Afghanistan remains one of the least developed countries in the world. But there are a few economic bright spots: fueled by aid, legal gross domestic product growth has been robust, and in 2010 the Karzai government increased revenue collection by 58 percent. Development programs such as the National Solidarity Program, which have exploited community councils and local decisionmaking, have been extremely successful. Local management means buy-in by the local population and great savings. In the 8 years of its existence, the NSP has affected 26,000 village communities with $631 million worth of projects.[16] The international community has agreed to funnel 50 percent of its annual aid through the Afghan state budget by 2012.[17] On Washington's end, the new ISAF COIN Contracting Guidance will help U.S. forces from indirectly contributing to local corruption.[18] By January 2011, the Afghan government had also aggressively begun to license the development of what may amount to $3 trillion worth of mineral deposits. In the long run, this mineral wealth could be a way out of underdevelopment for Afghanistan.[19]

Finally, the Afghan people are tired of war and the intrusive presence of coalition forces. While ISAF-involved civilian deaths and collateral damage were way down in 2010, the presence of coalition forces is no doubt hard for many Afghans to live with. Fortunately, for the most part, the people despise the Taliban more than the government and its coalition partners. The Taliban rarely receive higher than 10 percent approval ratings in polls. Most people seem able to remember how repressive and ineffective the Taliban was at ruling the country from 1996 to 2001. With 49 nations helping the government, the attentive public no doubt recalls that the Taliban regime was recognized by only 3 other countries. Before looking at policy options, it will therefore be helpful to discuss the international dimension of the conflict in Afghanistan.

The International Dimension

The interests of six regional players—China, India, Iran, Pakistan, Russia, and Saudi Arabia, each powerful in its own way—will have an important impact on the war and its settlement. Each of these nations will work hard to accomplish its own goals in and toward Afghanistan.

They are part of the policy milieu and in some cases part of the problem. They will all have to become part of the solution.

Russia has a long history with Afghanistan. It has legitimate commercial interests and is vitally interested in keeping radical Islamists away from its borders. Russia is also vitally concerned with preventing the spread of narcotics and the movement of drugs through its territory. It has long and deep relations with the numbers of the former Northern Alliance. It can be helpful in a settlement or it can be a spoiler. Afghanistan, for its part, might well see Russia as a source of security assistance, especially given the amount of former Warsaw Pact materiel in Kabul's armories.

India's prime interest is to spread its influence and keep Afghanistan from becoming a pawn of its enemy, Pakistan.[20] For decades, and especially since the November 2008 attacks in Mumbai, counterterrorism remains uppermost in the minds of Indian leaders. They see Pakistan as maintaining close relationships with a number of radical groups, including the Haqqani Network and Lashkar-i-Taiba, the latter singled out in a recent Council on Foreign Relations study as a potential rival to "al-Qaeda as the world's most sophisticated and dangerous terrorist organization."[21] India also keeps one eye on China, a close ally of Islamabad as well as India's rival for power in South Asia. For its part, China is exploiting its interests in Afghanistan for commercial reasons and to dampen Islamist extremism, a problem in the western part of China.

Not invited by Kabul to use military instruments in Afghanistan, New Delhi has committed over $1 billion in aid and pledged another $1 billion. It is fast improving its commercial ties, and Indian contractors and firms run many large projects inside the country. The Indian government no doubt maintains contacts with its old friends, the Tajiks and Uzbeks in northern Afghanistan. India has also linked up with Iran in bypassing Pakistani land routes into Afghanistan by improving the flow of supplies from the port of Charbahar in southeast Iran to Zaranj in Afghanistan, and then on to Delaram on the Ring Road in western Afghanistan. India has a secure route for its exports, which have Afghan trade preferences, and Iran is developing a close relationship with a highly regarded emerging power. Pakistan is concerned about the grow-ing demi-alliance between Iran and India, as well as the proximity of the commercial and maritime hub of Charbahar close to its own territory.

Islamabad's prime interest is to have a friendly, pliable regime in Af-ghanistan, which some of its strategists see as its strategic rear area, and also a regime that recognizes Pakistan's interests. As always, its sharpest eye is on India. Islamabad wants to block any extension of New Delhi's influence in Afghanistan. It also believes that India is actively undermining its security interests by using its extensive presence in Afghanistan to work with the Pakistani Taliban and Baluch insurgent groups. Islamabad has accordingly begun to cooperate more closely with the Afghan government.

Pakistan supported the Taliban until 2001, and then, pledges to the United States aside, allowed it to reoccupy sanctuaries inside Pakistan in Quetta, Karachi, the Federally Administered Tribal Areas, and through-out the northwest of Pakistan. The Pakistani leadership, however, is tiring of the Afghan Taliban, who maintain low-key relations with the Pakistani Taliban, which is currently at war with Islamabad. The Afghan Taliban in its various guises was once a solution to Pakistan's Afghanistan problem, but today it is an impediment to a new settlement. In the fall of 2010, with pressure from NATO, it appeared that the government of Pakistan had begun to push the Taliban toward negotiations with the Karzai gov-ernment. Although Islamabad has never had better cooperation with the current Afghan regime, it is no doubt hedging its bets for the future, worried about continuing instability, a vacuum left by a rapid departure of ISAF combat forces, and Indian gains in the country at the perceived expense of Pakistan's security.

The degree of help the coalition gets from Islamabad will be a key variable in fighting or negotiating with the Taliban. Increased Pakistani pressure on the Afghan Taliban could dramatically speed up reconciliation. The government of Pakistan, however, must cope with competing national objectives and a population in which "most Pakistanis will remain young, poor, uneducated and brimming with anti-Americanism."[22] The United States must continue to insist that Pakistan take action to control U.S. and Afghan enemies that reside on its soil.

For its part, Saudi Arabia is eager to facilitate reconciliation and continue its support for its old friend Pakistan, no doubt with one eye on Iran's activities. It has tried hard to jump-start the peace process in the hope of countering al Qaeda. Sadly, the Taliban has stiff-armed the Saudis on the al Qaeda issue. Saudi cash could be a great boon to reconciliation and a major aid source for Afghanistan.

Iran has had poor relations with the Taliban, which mistreated Shia Afghans and on one occasion killed Iranian consular officials in northern Afghanistan. Although it has provided some covert aid to the Taliban insurgents, it is not eager to have a Taliban government on its border. Tehran is also concerned about refugees, instability, and narcotics traffic across its porous border. At the same time, it does not want an American position of strength in Afghanistan, and it would love to see the war there become an embarrassment to the United States. Iran must also wonder whether Afghanistan would provide bases to the United States if a conflict were to arise over Iranian nuclear proliferation. Additionally,

Tehran is concerned about its long border with Afghanistan, cross-border instability, smuggling, and narcotics trafficking. Accordingly, it has a two-track policy of covert aid to insurgents and overt aid to Afghan authorities in Kabul and along Iran's eastern border. Shared interests have helped Tehran's relations with India grow stronger as the conflict continues.

In all, there is a tangle of competing interests and policies among the regional powers. The six big regional players, four of which are nuclear powers and one that is building that capability, will insist that any solution or reconciliation in Afghanistan does not work against their interests. To that end, an understanding among them on the future of Afghanistan will be critical to the country's long-term stability.

Options for the Future

Among the catalysts for strategic change in Afghanistan have been a surge of U.S. forces and civilian officials, increases in aid, and the President's declaration at West Point that in July 2011 "our troops will begin to come home." On that date, the coalition will start to transition responsibility for security in selected areas to the Afghan government. At the Lisbon Summit, NATO made 2014 the target for the Afghans to take over security nationwide. President Karzai first agreed to the 2014 date in the spring of 2010 and said as much at his appearance at the U.S. Institute of Peace.[23] President Obama and his Secretaries of State and Defense have all stressed that this withdrawal of combat forces will be "conditions based" and supplemented by a new strategic relationship with Afghanistan and Pakistan for the long term.

Four types of options will dominate the thought process in July 2011 and over the next few years. First, there will no doubt be some key players who favor continuing with the comprehensive COIN effort that is still unfolding. Many security specialists will prefer to keep up the full-blown counterinsurgency operation for a few more years and move slowly on the transition to Afghan responsibility for security, and only then on to reconciliation with the enemy. A few more years of the COIN approach would give the time needed for building Afghan capacity, but it would be expensive and play into enemy propaganda about the coalition as an occupying force. The Lisbon Summit goal of a transition to Afghan responsibility for security in 2014 favors a "more COIN" option, but expense, public opinion, and the ongoing budget deficit crunch will work against many more years of robust COIN efforts at the current level.

A second option touted by those interested primarily in al Qaeda or saving money is to abandon the complex counterinsurgency/nation-building focus and shift to a sole emphasis on counterterrorism. While counterterrorism has been an important part of option one, counterterrorism by itself does not work to strengthen the Afghan state so it can do business on its own. Without such help, the need for aid to Afghanistan will become unending. Absence of such help also retards the collection of local intelligence. Failing to secure the population will allow progress by insurgents and will also put forces engaged in counterterrorism in Afghanistan at higher personal risk. One highly sensitive assumption underpinning counterterrorism-only proposals is that there is a great dividing line between even the hardcore Taliban and al Qaeda. This is not the case. Many hardcore Taliban leaders are clearly found in the greater constellation of al Qaeda and its Associated Movements. This fact will be explored in depth in the next section. A final factor that would argue against a counterterrorism-only approach has been the strength of the kinetic operations inside Afghanistan and the aggressive drone attacks in Pakistan. The effectiveness of counterterrorist and counterguerrilla operations inside of the current COIN approach has been remarkable.

A third option would be to reduce over a few years many or most of the 30,000 Soldiers and Marines in the surge combat forces and make security assistance and capacity building—not the provision of combat forces—ISAF's top priority. Remaining ISAF combat units could further integrate with fielded ANA units. Maximum emphasis would be placed on quality training for soldiers and police.

To help build Afghan military capacity, ISAF commanders would also emphasize the development of Afghan combat enablers such as logistics, transportation, and aviation. In this option, ISAF would shift the focal point of allied strategy to the NATO Training Mission–Afghanistan vice allied combat forces. This option would not be cheap, but it could gradually bring down costs and troop levels. Trading U.S. combat units for ANA formations, however, may result in some short-term security degradation, a real problem if negotiations are ongoing. The integration of ISAF combat units with ANA units has paid great training dividends in just a few years. One more problem is the sustainment of ANSF funding. The current cost of the ANP and ANA is about five times the amount of all of Afghanistan's annual revenue. In the long run, the government will have to make serious adjustments to ensure that the ANSF can be supported with local revenues. Downsizing, conscription, and enhanced revenue collection could be among the potential fixes.

Other challenges may arise with this option. U.S. and allied trainer/advisor shortages will have to be filled rapidly, which will be difficult. In a similar vein, the training and education of Afghan civil servants will need much more attention along with additional trainer/advisors. To bring this about, the coalition also needs to reinforce support to the national government, its ministries, and its local appointees. Coalition civilian advisors must become the norm in every ministry and throughout their subdivisions.

The key to success here is and will remain the Afghan police, who will be vital to defeating the insurgency. Efforts to improve their training are essential. Rule of law programs such as courts, jails, and legal services must also be improved if this government will ever rival Taliban dispute resolution mechanisms. The Ministry of the Interior will have to defeat its endemic corruption. The appointment of General Bismillah Khan Mohammadi, formerly chief of the general staff, as the minister of the interior may provide a needed impetus for change. The development of the Afghan Local Police—trained by U.S. Special Forces, tied to local shuras, and supervised by the Ministry of the Interior—is both a favorable development and a challenge. By February 2011, there were over 30 districts, with nearly 10,000 local police in training or already validated.[24] As noted above, this program could easily become counterproductive without good training and supervision.

For its part, the government of Afghanistan—which ultimately must win its own war—must work harder against corruption and redouble its efforts to develop its own capacity in every field of endeavor. Links between the center and the provinces must be strengthened. The civilian part of the U.S. surge must clearly be maintained for a few more years.[25]

A Fourth Option: Reconciliation (and Its Obstacles)

A fourth option—compatible with the options noted above, either sequentially or concurrently—is for the Afghan government, with coalition and UN support, to move expeditiously on reintegration of individual Taliban fighters and reconciliation with parts of or even with whole elements of the Afghan Taliban. Over 1,000 individual fighters have volunteered for the reintegration program.[26] To make systemic progress, however, President Karzai first will have to win over the majority of the Afghan population who are not Pashtuns, a hard sell. They will want peace but not at a price that threatens them or allows a "new" Taliban much latitude. To help address this problem, President Karzai held a loya jirga on peace issues in June 2010. He wisely appointed Burhanuddin Rabbani, a Tajik and former Northern Alliance leader, to lead the High Peace Council. No Afghan will be able to accuse the Council of being biased toward certain individuals or Pashtun tribes.

For their part, the Taliban leadership will also be a hard sell. The year 2009 was the worst year for fighting since 2002. While they are feeling the heat in 2010, the Taliban still claim to have the momentum. The last few years have been a time of increasing Taliban battlefield successes and growing Western casualties. They have attacked cities, they exert control over some provinces, and they have shadow governors appointed for, but not necessarily working in, each province. Many in the Taliban leadership cadres are not eager to negotiate, but the U.S. surge and Pakistani pressure could change their minds.

While few would disagree with welcoming individual Taliban back into the fold, a political deal with the movement will be difficult to manage. If the Afghan government sits down prematurely with a major element of the Taliban, it may be acting from a position of weakness. To increase the prospects for Kabul's success in negotiating, the coalition will have to reverse that weakness. In plain language, ISAF will have to strike a decisive blow against the Taliban and fracture its organization while holding out the carrot of a settlement. Pakistan will have to join these efforts to push elements of the Taliban toward reconciliation.

Negotiators will have to deal with a number of complicating factors. For one, the Taliban has many factions. The original Taliban, the so-called Quetta Shura Taliban, works in the southern part of Afghanistan. Gulbuddin Hekmatyar's faction of Hezb-i-Islami, which has been at war in various configurations since 1978, operates in the eastern part of the country, as the does the Haqqani Network, whose headquarters is in North Waziristan. Complicating the issue, there are now multiple Pakistani Taliban factions, some operating in both countries. When we talk to the Taliban, we will have to deal with its many parts. The divisions among groups provide the coalition opportunities to use divide and conquer tactics. In the end, it is likely that some factions may reconcile while others fight on.

Second, all politics is local, and in Afghanistan that means ethnic or tribal. Pashtuns are only about 40 percent of the Afghan population, and the balance of the population—Tajiks, Uzbeks, and Hazaras, and others—were treated harshly by the Taliban. While Pashtuns may see some of the Taliban as wayward relatives, non-Pashtuns are likely to be less forgiving. A premature political reconciliation could increase Pashtun versus non-Pashtun tensions. The worst reconciliation nightmare would be a civil war with reconciled Pashtuns against nearly everyone else in Afghanistan. It will be hard to bring all of the ethnic groups on board, but war weariness and the need for development aid are powerful incentives to forgive and forget. Positive Pakistani efforts could increase Taliban motivation to reenter the political system.

Third, the Taliban regime also committed numerous crimes against humanity for which there has never been an accounting. In addition to the extreme repression of the entire citizenry including no kites, no music, no female education, bizarre human rights practices, and executions at soccer matches, thousands of Afghans, especially non-Pashtuns, were killed by the Taliban. Compounding that problem, the contemporary Taliban use terror tactics and repression. Even today, when they are trying to attract more followers with propaganda and sharia-based dispute resolution, their approval ratings in most polls are low.

While Karzai will demand that they accept the constitution, the Taliban reject democracy and may insist on a withdrawal of coalition forces, Karzai's insurance policy, before they sign on to reconciliation. Today's Taliban are unlawful combatants who live by planting IEDs, kidnapping civilians, and destroying reconstruction projects in the countryside. It will be difficult to sit down to negotiate with players whose signature tactics include burning girls' schools and beheading noncombatants. Even Mullah Omar has counseled restraint to soften the Taliban image.[27] Clearly, mainstream Taliban leaders will have to turn their back on their "worst practices."

Finally, there may be a tendency to see the Taliban as misguided fundamentalist bumpkins with their leadership cadres in a league with al Qaeda. Since 1998, they have resisted all requests to turn over or even disavow Osama bin Laden and his followers. In 2001, the Taliban were ousted from their home for protecting their "guest," Osama bin Laden, with his thousands of foreign fighters. While al Qaeda was once a more powerful partner, it is still able to advise Taliban commanders and teach them the finer points of IEDs and suicide bombing techniques. The al Qaeda–Taliban link may be stronger today than it was in 2001.

According to Dexter Filkins writing in the *New York Times*, no less a figure than Saudi Arabia's King Abdullah in the summer of 2008 asked Mullah Omar to disavow in writing a link between the Taliban and al Qaeda. He never received an answer.[28] David Rohde of the *New York Times*, who was kidnapped by the Haqqani Network for 7 months, believes the al Qaeda–Taliban link is thriving. Rohde wrote in October 2009:

> *Over those months* [in captivity], *I came to a simple realization. After seven years of reporting in the region, I did not fully understand how extreme many of the Taliban had become. Before the kidnapping, I viewed the organization as a form of "Al Qaeda lite," a religiously motivated movement primarily focused on controlling Afghanistan. Living side by side with the Haqqanis' followers, I learned that the goal of the hard-line Taliban was far more ambitious. Contact with foreign militants in the tribal areas appeared to have deeply affected many young Taliban fighters. They wanted to create a fundamentalist Islamic emirate with Al Qaeda that spanned the Muslim world.*[29]

Peter Bergen, an expert on al Qaeda, sees the issue in a similar fashion. For him the Taliban, Afghan and Pakistani, are brothers in arms with al Qaeda. In a 2009 article in the *New Republic* he wrote:

> *But, in recent years, Taliban leaders have drawn especially close to Al Qaeda. (There are basically two branches of the Taliban — Pakistani and Afghan — but both are currently head-quartered in Pakistan, and they are quite a bit more interwoven*

than is commonly thought.) Today, at the leadership level, the Taliban and Al Qaeda function more or less as a single entity. The signs of this are everywhere. For instance, IED attacks in Afghanistan have increased dramatically since 2004. What happened? As a Taliban member told Sami Yousafzai and Ron Moreau of Newsweek, *"The Arabs taught us how to make an IED by mixing nitrate fertilizer and diesel fuel and how to pack plastic explosives and to connect them to detonators and remote-control devices like mobile phones. We learned how to do this blindfolded so we could safely plant IEDs in the dark." Another explained that "Arab and Iraqi mujahedin began visiting us, transferring the latest IED technology and suicide-bomber tactics they had learned in the Iraqi resistance." Small numbers of Al Qaeda instructors embedded with much larger Taliban units have functioned something like U.S. Special Forces do, as trainers and force multipliers.*[30]

A mid-level official affiliated with both the Afghan and Pakistani Taliban, Mawlawi Omar, with perhaps a drop or two of exaggeration, trumpeted the unity of the Taliban and al Qaeda in a 2008 interview with Claudio Franco, an Italian regional specialist and journalist:

There is no difference between Al Qaeda and the Taliban. The formation of Al Qaeda and the Taliban was based on an ideology. Today, Taliban and Al Qaeda have become an ideology. Whoever works for these organizations, they fight against Kafirs [unbelievers]. . . . However, those fighting in foreign countries are called Al Qaeda while those fighting in Afghanistan and Pakistan are called Taliban. In fact, both are the name of one ideology. The aim and objectives of both organizations are the same.[31]

To be successful, reconciliation will have to practice "divide and conquer" and shatter the Taliban as an alliance of organizations. It will be the segments of the Taliban willing to disavow al Qaeda, along with the disgruntled, war-weary field cadres, who will meet the requirements for reconciliation. The death of Osama bin Laden at the hands of Navy SEALs in May 2011 may well accelerate reconciliation, but the bond between the Taliban and al Qaeda leadership is ideological as well as personal. Difficult as it will be, however, reconciliation has significant support and political momentum. Irregular conflicts rarely end in a surrender ceremony on a battleship, as World War II did, or with one side decisively defeating the other, as in the Vietnam War. Political compromises and negotiated settlements are the norm. Some last, and some do not. The Afghan government and its enemies know this history well. It will take years to set the conditions and conduct negotiations that lead to a lasting settlement.

To proceed systematically in Afghanistan, the United States and its coalition partners have to first reinforce the foundation for reconciliation efforts. To achieve favorable conditions for negotiations, ISAF must continue to accelerate its military efforts. General David Petraeus is correct: ISAF cannot kill or capture its way to victory in Afghanistan. Its forces must focus on protecting the population. At the same time, however, ISAF can create an enemy more eager to negotiate if it defeats Taliban offensive operations, destroys its field forces, dries up its means of support, damages its fundraising, disrupts the narcotics trade, and threatens its sanctuaries. Pakistan's help can magnify the effects of ISAF's efforts.

In the short run, large numbers of Afghan and NATO troops, as well as more civilian advisors and aid money, will be essential. In other words, the United States and its coalition partners must carry out President Obama's plan and pursue the enemy ruthlessly, rigorously, and continuously. Cutting off Taliban funds and support will be as important as destroying its cadres on the battlefield. The biggest mistake the coalition could make would be to slack off on the battlefield while the Taliban plays the talk-fight card.

In preparing for the future, the NATO nations must also continue to build Afghan police and military capacity for independent operations. We have done better at this in Iraq than in Afghanistan, but Iraq had more human capital and more sustained U.S. resources. Progress in building police and army formations was very impressive in 2010.[32] Building across-the-board Afghan capacity for governance and management must also be a top long-term priority. In the end, better training and an increase in more military and civilian advisors may be more important than additional U.S. brigade combat teams.

At long last, Pakistan seems ready to pressure the Afghan Taliban and help with reconciliation. Beset by its own Taliban insurgents, the Pakistani leadership may well have concluded that a Taliban-dominated Afghanistan is not in its interest. The government in Islamabad is no doubt eager to be shut of the radical Taliban. Again, more aid for Pakistan — military and economic — must be part of the reconciliation program, especially in the wake of the summer flooding in 2010. Working toward a long-term strategic partnership remains an important element in the equation.

Reconciliation and attendant negotiations are issues on which the Afghan government must lead. We cannot navigate the maze of Afghanistan's ethnic politics. Only the Afghan leadership can do that, and it has been one of President Karzai's abiding strengths. One theme for our public diplomacy should be that the United States is in Afghanistan for the long haul—it will be there for years beyond the end of all major fighting. Another key theme should be continued support for Afghanistan while our combat troops are there as well as after they leave. U.S. diplomats have done a good job of emphasizing these themes. As long as the coalition is in Kabul, the Taliban knows it cannot force its way in. It must be made to believe that reconciliation is its best hope.

Political reconciliation between the Afghan government and the Taliban (or any of its factions or field forces) should require the Taliban participants to accept a number of key conditions. The Taliban must verifiably lay down its arms. It must accept the Afghan constitution and agree to operate within it. It must also forsake the criminal enterprises that have become its lifeline and pledge to become a legitimate political entity inside Afghanistan. There should be no offers of territorial power sharing or extra constitutional arrangements, but later on the president might appoint Taliban cabinet officers or provincial or district governors. Taliban fighters could clearly be integrated into the ethnically integrated Afghan security forces after retraining and indoctrination.

Reintegration and reconciliation, first with individual fighters and then with elements of the Taliban, will be difficult but not impossible. It represents a potential way to end the 33 years of war that have beset this land. It will require great Western political, military, and economic effort during the reconciliation period and close attention to U.S.-Afghan relations in the long-term future. The cooperation of regional partners, especially Pakistan, will be critical. This process is likely to take years, but it carries with it the promise of the first peace in Afghanistan in over three decades.

In sterile decisionmaking exercises, teams might well decide that the safest way to proceed would be to go through these four options in order, starting with another dose of robust counterinsurgency programs, with coincident reintegration of individual belligerents. This would be followed by "Afghanization," with reconciliation beginning only after option two is well underway. However, this is a time of rapid change on many fronts. Reconciliation, spurred by political maneuvering and war weariness, may end up leading and not following developments on the battlefield. Counterinsurgency successes in Pakistan can change the battlefield dynamics in Afghanistan and vice versa. Agreements among regional powers can affect military operations. The exploitation of mineral wealth may provide great incentives for some insurgents to come home and improve their economic lot.

There is an understandable reluctance to move into negotiations while the war continues, but as noted above, most irregular and civil wars end in some form of negotiation, often after a decade or more of fighting. The United States should not stand in the way of reconciliation with the Taliban. Rather, it should work for the best possible outcome, guided by its objectives, the available means, and the strategic context.

10. Conclusion

It is not possible now to chart an exact course for the future. Despite one's best hopes, the war may continue unabated. A Taliban victory, with black turbaned fighters triumphantly riding their pickup trucks into Kabul, is highly unlikely and nearly impossible unless the West abandons the Afghan regime. Allied success, however, may take many paths. Security assistance may move to the forefront of the allied agenda, allowing for the withdrawal of some or all of ISAF's combat forces. Reintegration of individuals and reconciliation with part or all of the Taliban may occur much faster than the Western powers expect. Afghanistan's history is replete with examples where entire armed factions change sides in recognition of new realities. Regional actors such as Pakistan or even Iran may play more constructive roles in reaching settlements or otherwise fashioning a better peace.

While major outcomes are uncertain, there are a number of key issues that the U.S. leadership team needs to tackle right away. First, on the military end, it will be necessary to keep up the pressure on the Taliban. Protecting the population should remain the first priority, but one of the best ways to do that is to eliminate the Taliban, whose forces oppress the population the coalition seeks to safeguard. If reconciliation advances, there will be many, including some in Afghanistan and Pakistan, who will want to cut back on offensive operations and counterterrorist activities against the Taliban and al Qaeda. In truth, reconciliation in the long run depends on destroying Taliban formations, fracturing the Taliban alliance, and convincing many of its constituent commanders that reconciliation is a better path.

Secondly, it is clear that there needs to be a high level of civil-military teamwork throughout the U.S. leadership in country, both in the capital and in the field. Iraq and Afghanistan are proof positive that personal chemistry can remove obstacles to cooperation but that the chemistry is not always there. You cannot legislate or direct such chemistry, but clarifying intracommand relationships may help. The civilian surge is working. With over 1,000 U.S. Government civilians in country, there is now integration of politico-military efforts at the brigade, regional, district-province, and national levels.[1] Civil and military leaders at the regional command and brigade levels may well be ahead of their Washington and Kabul-based superiors in forging adaptive whole-of-government approaches to problems in Afghanistan. Ambassadors Ryan Crocker and Marc Grossman will have their work cut out for them.

Third, the coalition needs to work not harder but smarter on the narcotics problem.[2] Profits or "taxes" from the narcotics trade fund the Taliban and corrupt government officials. Addiction and drug use are a growing problem in the region, even in the Afghan National Security Forces. ISAF should continue to increase its efforts, not against farmers but drug lords, warehouses, and laboratories. When the drug lord infrastructure is gone, eradication will become easier and crop substitution will have a real chance.[3]

Fourth, the United States should develop a regional strategy for South Asia that in the long run restores appropriate priorities. T.X. Hammes and former U.S. Ambassador to Pakistan Robert Oakley, both distinguished National Defense University scholars, have reminded us of an opportunity cost of the current war in Afghanistan that few have mentioned:

The focus on the war in Afghanistan has prevented the United States from developing a South Asia strategy rooted in the relative strategic importance of the nations in the region. India, a

*stable democracy enjoying rapid growth, clearly has the most po-
tential as a strategic partner. Pakistan, as the home of al Qaeda
leadership and over 60 nuclear weapons, is the greatest threat to
regional stability and growth. Yet Afghanistan absorbs the vast
majority of U.S. effort in the region. The United States needs to
develop a genuine regional strategy.*[4]

The authors recommend greater attention to political reform and
economic development in Pakistan, as well as increased attention to
building trust between New Delhi and Islamabad. Long-term postconflict relationships in South and Southwest Asia must be a priority for our
diplomats and strategic planners. Peace between India and Pakistan is
as important for the United States as peace between Israel and its neighbors. Solving the conflict in Afghanistan could be a first link in a chain
of peace in the region.

Finally, the United States, its allies, and the international financial
institutions need to focus on building Afghan capacity, not just in the
short term in the national security ministries, but across the board in the
civil government and private sectors. Training and advising Afghan security forces are important immediate steps, but we must think in terms of
decades about how to help Afghanistan help itself overcome the effects
of 33 years of war. The West must reinforce training and advisory efforts
that help the Afghan government improve governance, rule of law, and
basic enterprise management. U.S. educational institutions should be
encouraged to reach out to Afghan colleges and graduate schools to help
modernize them. While working more closely with province and district
governments is important, it is also true that there will be no end to the
problems of Afghanistan unless there is a functioning government in

Kabul that is linked into the provinces and districts and able to perform the basic security and welfare functions of a state. A modicum of nation-building in Afghanistan is in the interest of the United States and its coalition partners. Even more important is to build Afghan capacity to develop Afghanistan. In that regard, the new NATO Training Mission–Afghanistan program for literacy training for Afghan enlisted soldiers may be a model for others engaged in building capacity in nonmilitary sectors. Along with capacity-building, harnessing and empowering local communities will be imperative. People-powered programs, such as the National Solidarity Program, are key to good governance and local development.

The United States has for a decade argued in its advisory and development activities that "teaching people how to fish is better than giving them fish." The truth of the matter is, however, that the United States is superb at providing fish and not very good at teaching people how to fish, which in this case means building capacity and mentoring. As we work on building national security and local defense forces, we need to redouble our efforts at building up Afghan human capital and the institutions of governance that one day will enable the state to stand on its own two feet as a decent and effective government. If this does not come to pass, the United States and its allies will ultimately fail in Afghanistan.[5]

Suggestions for Further Reading

A number of works are available for those interested in going deeper into the study of war in Afghanistan. General history should be the first stop. I am partial to Martin Ewans, *Afghanistan: A Short History of Its People and Politics*, published by Harper Perennial, 2002. A well-regarded more recent work from the Princeton University Press, 2010, is Thomas Barfield's *Afghanistan: A Cultural and Political History*. Barfield is both an area expert and an anthropologist, and these qualifications add a unique perspective to his work. The political economy of Afghanistan is also important. The premier source for this sort of enquiry is Barnett Rubin, *The Fragmentation of Afghanistan: State Formation and Collapse in the International System*, Yale University Press, 1995 and 2001. Larry Goodson's *Afghanistan's Endless War: State Failure, Regional Politics, and the Rise of the Taliban*, University of Washington Press, 2001, covers a good bit of history and puts Afghanistan's problems as a failed state in a broader theoretical context. The 9-hour series of plays by the United Kingdom's Tricycle Theater Company entitled *The Great Game*, directed by Nicolas Kent and Indhu Rubasingham, is a moving educational experience that will enlighten viewers on a broad range of historical problems from 19th-century wars through 21st-century problems. The plays also help viewers to see local issues through Afghan eyes. On the Soviet-Afghan war, see Henry Bradsher, *Afghanistan and the Soviet Union*, from Duke University Press, 1983, and Lester Grau, *The Bear Went Over the Mountain*, NDU Press, 1995. Diego Cordovez and Selig Harrison's *Out of Afghanistan*, Oxford University Press, 1995, does an excellent job of covering peacemaking in that war.

Understanding the lives of contemporary Afghans would be a fruitful second step. Sarah Chayes, *Punishment of Virtue: Inside Afghanistan After the Taliban*, Penguin Press, 2006, is the story of an American journalist living, working, and observing tribal politics among the Kandaharis in the early post-Taliban years. Asne Seierstad's *The Bookseller of Kabul* from Back Bay Books, 2004, is concerned with traditional family life as experienced by a progressive Kabuli. The popular novels by Khaled Hosseini, *The Kite Runner* and *A Thousand Splendid Suns*, are both entertaining and educational for Western audiences.

Those interested in the current fighting should first learn more about the Taliban. Steve Coll's encyclopedic *Ghost Wars*, Penguin Press, 2004, covers the waterfront from the late 1970s to 2001. Pakistani author Ahmed Rashid's *Taliban*, originally published in 2000 by Yale University Press, and its sequel *Descent into Chaos: The United States and the Failure of Nation Building in Pakistan, Afghanistan, and Central Asia*, from Viking-Penguin, 2008, are both topnotch. A more up-to-date analysis of the Taliban can be found in an anthology edited by Antonio Giustozzi, *Decoding the New Taliban: Insights from the Afghan Field*, published by Columbia University Press, 2009. Also published by Columbia, Abdul Salam Zaeff, a former Taliban ambassador and current peace activist, wrote *My Life with the Taliban*, translated and edited by Alex Strick van Linschoten and Felix Kuehn. If the reader can wade through the propaganda, exaggeration, and omissions, he can gain insight into how senior Taliban officials think. One of the best treatments of al Qaeda's strategy in Afghanistan is Bruce Reidel's *The Search for Al Qaeda*, 2008 and 2010, Brookings Institution Press. Reidel is a former CIA executive who is now a scholar at the Brookings Institution in Washington, DC.

For more about the current conflict, two "graveyard of empires" books are among the best out there: Seth Jones, *In the Graveyard of Empires: America's War in Afghanistan* from Current Affairs-Norton, 2009, and David Isby, *Afghanistan, Graveyard of Empires: A New History of the Borderlands* from Pegasus Books, 2010. The current conflict is fueled by the growth, distribution, sales, and "taxes" from illegal narcotics, particularly opium and hashish. No student should go forth to this war zone, literally or virtually, without having read Gretchen Peters's *Seeds of Terror: How Heroin Is Bankrolling the Taliban and Al Qaeda*, published by Thomas Dunne–St. Martin's, 2009. On the diplomacy of this war, James Dobbins's *After the Taliban, Nation-Building in Afghanistan*, Potomac Books, 2008, gives the inside story of the formation of the new Afghan state. On pre-surge diplomacy, Ronald Neumann's *The Other War: Winning and Losing in Afghanistan*, Potomac Books, 2009, provides an invaluable record from one of America's most seasoned diplomats. For those with a yen for metrics, the first stop should be Brookings's *Afghanistan Index*, published quarterly on their Web site, <http://www.brookings.edu/foreign-policy/afghanistan-index.aspx>, under the direction of Ian Livingston, Heather Messera, and Michael E. O'Hanlon. For day-to-day reporting, don't miss The New America Foundation's *Af-Pak Channel Daily Brief*, edited by Katherine Tidemann and available on the *Foreign Policy* Web site, <http://afpak.foreignpolicy.com/dailybrief>.

There is a rich and important literature on Pakistan. In addition to the books by Coll and Rashid, noted above, I would recommend Pakistani Ambassador to the United States Husain Haqqani, *Pakistan: Beteween Mosque and Military*, published by the Carnegie Endowment for International Peace, 2005. Marvin Weinbaum and Shuja Nawaz are also leaders in Pakistan studies. For our purposes, two of their essential works are Marvin Weinbaum's *Afghanistan and Its Neighbors*, published by United States Institute of Peace in 2006, and Shuja Nawaz's *Crossed Swords: Pakistan, Its Army, and the Wars Within*, published by Oxford University Press in 2008. Bruce Reidel's *Deadly Embrace: Pakistan, America, and the Future of the Global Jihad*, Brookings Institution Press, 2011, is short and insightful.

The functional areas of counterinsurgency and nation-building should not be neglected. On counterinsurgency, the U.S. Army/Marine Corps *Counterinsurgency Field Manual*, published by the University of Chicago Press, 2007, should be a first reference. T.X. Hammes's *The Sling and the Stone*, published by Zenith Press, 2006, and David Kilcullen's *Accidental Guerrilla*, published by Oxford University Press, 2009, are both excellent and bring classical notions of insurgency into the 21st century. Also important is the Army's new field manual on the softer side of counterinsurgency, FM 3–07, *Stability Operations*, published by the University of Michigan Press, 2009. The origins of the Army's efforts to learn about COIN and stability operations are explored in Janine Davidson, *Lifting the Fog of Peace: How Americans Learned to Fight Modern War*, University of Michigan Press, 2010. Experts in counterinsurgency also speak well of *Counterinsurgency in Modern Warfare*, a recent volume edited by Daniel Marston and Carter Malkasian. The dozen or so cases in the Marston-Malkasian volume present a deep set of lessons and analogies for the practitioner to draw on. Last but not least, those interested in COIN may wish to dig into the literature on current fighting in Afghanistan. Two books stand head and shoulders above the rest. Sebastian Junger's *War*, published by Hachette Book Group in 2010, covers fierce fighting in the Korengal Valley and is the basis for the award-winning film *Restrepo*. Bing West's *The*

Wrong War: Grit, Strategy, and the Way Out of Afghanistan (Random House, 2011), like Junger's book, is an eyewitness account of infantry combat in Afghanistan. West is a former combat Marine and former senior Pentagon official, and his book is a must for military people.

On the trials and tribulations of nation-building, a good first stop would be the series of RAND publications, done under the supervision of Ambassador James Dobbins. Novices will find two of them very useful: James Dobbins et al., *The Beginner's Guide to Nation-Building*, 2007; and James Dobbins et al., *America's Role in Nation-Building: From Germany to Iraq*, 2003.

Dov Zakheim covers the politics of budgets and resources in Washington in *A Vulcan's Tale: How the Bush Administration Mismanaged the Reconstruction of Afghanistan* (Brookings Institution, 2011).

Beyond these books noted above, the reader will find many interesting sources in the notes for this volume.

Notes

Opening Thoughts

[1] Ronald E. Neumann, *The Other War: Winning and Losing in Afghanistan* (Washington, DC: Potomac Books, 2009), 217.

[2] Eric Edelman, *Understanding America's Contested Primacy* (Washington, DC: Center for Strategic and Budgetary Assessment, 2010), 77.

Introduction

[1] This work relies heavily on Joseph J. Collins, *The Soviet Invasion of Afghanistan: A Study in the Use of Force in Soviet Foreign Policy* (Lexington, MA: Lexington Books, 1986); "Afghanistan: The Path to Victory," *Joint Force Quarterly* 54 (3d Quarter, 2009), available at <http://www.ndu.edu/press/lib/images/jfq-54/16.pdf>; "No Reason to Quit: Afghanistan Requires Our Greater Effort and Will, Not Less," *Armed Forces Journal* 147, no. 3, October 2009, available at <http://www.armedforcesjournal.com/2009/10/4266860/>; "Afghan Reconciliation," *Armed Forces Journal*, March 2010, available at <http://www.armedforcesjournal.com/2010/03/4491210/>; and "The Way Ahead in Afghanistan," *Armed Forces Journal*, July 2010, available at <http://www.armedforcesjournal.com/2010/07/4653525>.

Chapter 1

[1] The best readily available sources for geographic, economic, and demographic information on Afghanistan are U.S. Department of State, *Background Note: Afghanistan*, March 2010, available at <http://www.state.gov/r/pa/ei/bgn/5380.htm>; and Central Intelligence Agency, *The World Factbook*, pages on Afghanistan, October 2010, available at <https://www.cia.gov/library/publications/the-world-factbook/geos/af.html>.

[2] U.S. Institute of Peace (USIP), "Remarks with Afghan President Hamid Karzai in a Moderated Conversation" [with Secretary Hillary Clinton and Ambassador William Taylor, the moderator], May 13, 2010, available at <http://www.state.gov/secretary/rm/2010/05/141825.htm>. The U.S. Geological Service estimates the value at $1 trillion.

[3] I first heard Lieutenant General Eikenberry say this in 2005 both in Kabul and in Washington, DC.

[4] For a standard source on modern-day Pashtun tribal issues, see Tom Johnson and M. Chris Mason, "No Sign until the Burst of Fire: Understanding the Pakistan-Afghanistan Frontier," *International Security* 32, no. 4 (Spring 2008), 41–77.

[5] See Thomas Barfield, *Afghanistan: A Cultural and Political History* (Princeton, NJ: Princeton University Press, 2010), 26–27.

[6] Louis Dupree, *Afghanistan* (Princeton, NJ: Princeton University Press, 1980), 125–127.

[7] Ahmed Rashid, *Taliban: Militant Islam, Oil, and Fundamentalism in Central Asia*, 2d ed. (New Haven, CT: Yale University Press, 2000), 32.

[8] On Abdur Rahman Khan, the Iron Emir, see Martin Ewans, *Afghanistan: A Short History of Its People and Politics* (New York: Harper Perennial, 2002), 98–111. The quotation can be found in Dupree, *Afghanistan*, 415.

Chapter 2

[1] The rivalry between eastern and southern Pashtuns is highlighted in Barfield.

[2] Troop strength for the "Army of the Indus" from ibid., 114.

[3] For a précis of the Anglo-Afghan wars, see ibid., 111–163; and Ewans, *Afghanistan: A Short History*, 59–117. On how Abdur Rahman Khan ruled and how he used the subsidy, see Barnett Rubin, *The Fragmentation of Afghanistan: State Formation and Collapse in the International System* (New Haven, CT: Yale University Press, 1995), 48–53.

[4] Rudyard Kipling, "The Young British Soldier," available at <http://www.theotherpages.org/poems/kiplin11.html>.

[5] Ewans, 118–119.

[6] On the civil war, see Barfield, 188–195.

[7] U.S. Embassy, Kabul, *Policy Review: A U.S. Strategy for the '70s*, 1, annex, June 1971. Emphasis in the original has been removed. Similar formulations were repeated up until the late 1970s. See also analysis in Henry S. Bradsher, *Afghanistan and the Soviet Union*, 1st ed. (Durham, NC: Duke University Press, 1983), 51–52.

[8] Rubin, 52.

[9] Larry Goodson, *Afghanistan's Endless War: State Failure, Regional Politics, and the Rise of the Taliban* (Seattle: University of Washington Press, 2001), 25.

Chapter 3

[1] For an eyewitness analysis of the coup, see Louis Dupree, "Red Flag Over the Hindu Kush, Part II: The Accidental Coup or Taraki in Blunderland," *American Universities Field Staff Review*, no. 45, September 1979.

[2] Patrick Garrity, "The Soviet Military Stake in Afghanistan: 1956–1979," *Journal of the Royal United Services Institute* (September 1980), 33.

[3] Working Transcript of the Meeting of the Politburo, *Re: Deterioriation of the Conditions in DRA and Possible Responses from Our Side*, March 17, 1979. This document can be found in the Storage Center for Contemporary Documentation, Moscow, Fond 89, Perechen 25, Dokument 1. The English translation was done under the auspices of the Norwegian Nobel Institute for their 1995 Nobel Symposium, Oslo, September 1995.

[4] For an excellent summary of Soviet decisionmaking on the invasion based largely on declassified documents, see Diego Cordovez and Selig Harrison, *Out of Afghanistan: The Inside Story of the Soviet Withdrawal* (New York: Oxford University Press, 1995), 35–49.

[5] Central Committee of the Communist Party of the Soviet Union Memorandum, *Subject: Regarding Events in Afghanistan during 27–28 December 1979*, number 2519–A, dated December 31, 1979, 1. This document can be found in the Storage Center for Contemporary Documentation, Moscow, Fond 89, Perechen 42, Dokument 10. The English translation here was done under the auspices of the Norwegian Nobel Institute for their 1995 Nobel Symposium, Oslo, September 1995.

[6] On the salience of the year 1979, see Dan Caldwell, *Vortex of Conflict: U.S. Policy Toward Afghanistan, Pakistan and Iraq* (Stanford, CA: Stanford University Press, 2011), 23–26.

[7] Some sources put the highest Soviet troop strength at 115,000. On invasion and subsequent fighting, see Collins, *The Soviet Invasion of Afghanistan*, 77–164, and Bradsher, 169–239; on Soviet tactics, Lester Grau, ed., *The Bear Went Over the Mountain: Soviet Combat Tactics in Afghanistan* (Washington, DC: National Defense University Press, 1995); and on mujahideen tactics, Ali Ahmad Jalali and Lester Grau, *The Other Side of the Mountain: Mujahidin Tactics in the Soviet-Afghan War* (Quantico, VA: Marine Corps Combat Development Command, 1998).

[8] Bruce Reidel, *Deadly Embrace: Pakistan, America, and the Future of the Global Jihad* (Washington, DC: Brookings Institution, 2011), 27.

[9] Collins, *The Soviet Invasion of Afghanistan*, 145.

[10] For a précis of all of the Peshawar Seven groups, see Goodson, 189–193.

[11] See, for example, Artemy Kalinovsky, "Afghanistan Is the New Afghanistan," *Foreign Policy*, September 2009, available at <http://www.foreignpolicy.com/articles/2009/09/04/afghanistan_is_the_new_afghanistan>.

[12] Two excellent books about contemporary war in Afghanistan use "graveyard of empires" in their titles. David Isby, *Afghanistan, Graveyard of Empires: A New History of the Borderlands* (New York: Pegasus Books, 2010); and Seth Jones, *In the Graveyard of Empires: America's War in Afghanistan* (New York: W.W. Norton, 2009).

[13] There are also articles trumpeting the Vietnam-Afghanistan parallel. For one example, see Tom Johnson and M. Chris Mason, "Saigon 2009," *Foreign Policy*, August 20, 2009, available at <http://www.foreignpolicy.com/articles/2009/08/20/saigon_2009>. The Vietnam analogy does not carry water where the scope and scale of the conflict are concerned. Another anomalous item in that comparison is the salience of Soviet and Chinese security assistance and the existence of a massive and highly professional North Vietnamese army. This modern, mechanized army was the final instrument of defeat for the South Vietnamese government, not indigenous South Vietnamese guerrillas. There is no such factor in the current conflict in Afghanistan.

[14] Brookings Institution, *Afghanistan Index*, October 2010, figure 4.12, shows Taliban approval ratings totaling 10 percent; available at <http://www.brookings.edu/~/media/Files/Programs/FP/afghanistan%20index/index.pdf>. The strength of today's Taliban is the author's estimate, based on conversations with various intelligence analysts. On current Taliban troop strength, see the Associated Press story by Slobodan Lekic, "Taliban Numbers Unaffected by Allied Troop Surge," *Boston Globe*, January 7, 2010, available at <http://www.boston.com/news/world/europe/articles/2011/01/07/taliban_numbers_unaffected_by_allied_troop_surge/>.

Chapter 4

[1] For a short but excellent account of Najibullah's competition with the mujahideen, see Ewans, 238–260.

[2] Ibid., 252.

[3] Rashid, 27–28.

[4] Evans, 255.

[5] Grisly pictures of Najibullah's demise can be found in ibid., plate 34, near page 149.

[6] Goodson puts the percentage of terrain controlled by the Northern Alliance at only 3 to 10 percent of the country. Goodson, 86.

[7] Olivier Roy as quoted in Donald Wright et al., *A Different Kind of War: The U.S. Army in Operation Enduring Freedom*, October 2001–2005 (Fort Leavenworth, KS: Combat Studies Institute Press, May 2010), 19.

[8] As broadcast on Radio Sharia, Kabul, and recorded in Asne Seierstad, *The Bookseller of Kabul* (New York: Back Bay Books, 2003), 80–83.

[9] A summary on the zoo can be found in *National Geographic News*, June 10, 2002, available at <http://news.nationalgeographic.com/news/2002/06/0610_020610_kabulzoo_2.html>.

[10] For a concise assessment of sociocultural change under the Taliban, see Goodson, 127–132.

[11] On Osama bin Laden in Afghanistan, see Lawrence Wright, *The Looming Tower: Al-Qaeda and the Road to 9/11* (New York: Alfred Knopf, 2006), 99–120.

[12] On Osama in Sudan and Afghanistan, see ibid., 145–300.

[13] Reidel, *Deadly Embrace*, 55. Citing Gilles Doronsoro, Reidel claims that bin Laden married one of Mullah Omar's daughters. Other books regard the marriage as an unsubstantiated claim. See William Maley, *The Afghanistan Wars*, 2d ed. (London: Palgrave MacMillan, 2009), 213.

[14] Jones, 93.

[15] *The 9/11 Commission Report: Final Report of the National Commission on Terrorist Attacks Upon the United States* (New York: W.W. Norton and Co., 2004), 67.

[16] The fatwa is analyzed in Bernard Lewis, "License to Kill: Osama bin Ladin's Declaration of Jihad," *Foreign Affairs* (November/December 1998), available at <http://www.foreignaffairs.com/articles/54594/bernard-lewis/license-to-kill-usama-bin-ladins-declaration-of-jihad>.

[17] Ibid.

[18] *The 9/11 Commission Report*, 116–117.

[19] Ibid., 66.

Chapter 5

[1] A version of a complete al Qaeda strategy is laid out in Bruce Reidel, *The Search for Al Qaeda: Its Leadership, Ideology, and Future* (Washington, DC: Brookings Institution, 2010), 121–133. Reidel believes that al Qaeda sought as a first strategic step to entice the United States to engage in "bleeding wars" in Afghanistan and Iraq.

[2] For the full text of the Public Law 107–40, passed by the 107th Congress, "To authorize the use of United States Armed Forces against those responsible for the recent attacks launched against the United States," September 18, 2001, see <http://www.gpo.gov/fdsys/pkg/PLAW-107publ40/html/PLAW-107publ40.htm>.

[3] James Dobbins (Ambassador), *After the Taliban: Nation-Building in Afghanistan* (Washington, DC: Potomac Books, 2008), 47.

[4] The author acknowledges help on understanding Pakistani thinking from Dr. Thomas F. Lynch III of NDU's Institute for National Strategic Studies.

[5] For an interesting look at the early war, see Stephen Biddle, "Afghanistan and the Future of Warfare," *Foreign Affairs* (May 2003), available at <http://www.foreignaffairs.com/articles/58811/stephen-biddle/afghanistan-and-the-future-of-warfare>.

[6] Remarks by U.S. Secretary of Defense Donald Rumsfeld, National Defense University, Fort Lesley J. McNair, Washington, DC, January 31, 2002, available at <http://www.defense.gov/speeches/speech.aspx?speechid=183>.

[7] The best critical work on this subject is Sean Naylor, *Not a Good Day to Die: The Untold Story of Operation Anaconda* (New York: Berkley Books, 2005). The Army's official assessment can be found in Donald Wright et al., 127–179.

[8] Jones, 127.

[9] For the full text of the December 2001 Bonn Agreement, formally known as the *Agreement on Provisional Arrangements in Afghanistan Pending the Re-Establishment of Permanent Government Institutions*, see <http://www.afghangovernment.com/AfghanAgreementBonn.htm>.

[10] For an inside account of the Bonn process, see Dobbins, 51–97. For an account of life in Kandahar in the early postwar period and dominance of local warlords, see Sarah Chayes, *The Punishment of Virtue: Inside Afghanistan after the Taliban* (New York: Penguin Press, 2006).

[11] The current United Nations Security Council Resolution 1943, October 13, 2010, is available at <http://www.un.org/Docs/sc/unsc_resolutions10.htm>.

[12] James Dobbins et al., *America's Role in Nation-Building: From Germany to Iraq* (Santa Monica, CA: RAND, 2003), 156–159.

Chapter 6

[1] As reported in FM 3–24 Marine Corps Warfighting Publication 3–33.5, *Counterinsurgency* (Chicago: University of Chicago Press, 2007), paragraph 1-2, 2. All subsequent citations to this document will be the University of Chicago Press version.

[2] Robert Taber, *War of the Flea: The Classical Study of Guerrilla Warfare* (Washington, DC: Brassey's, Inc., 2002), 20.

[3] The most basic text was by Mao Zedong, trans. Samuel B. Griffith II, *On Guerrilla Warfare* (Urbana: University of Illinois Press, 2000).

[4] The best analysis of the typology of insurgency can be found in Bard E. O'Neill, *Insurgency and Terrorism: From Revolution to Apocalypse*, 2ᵈ ed., revised (Washington, DC: Potomac Books, 2005).

[5] David Galula, *Counterinsurgency Warfare: Theory and Practice* (Westport, CT: Praeger, 2006), 63.

[6] Ibid., 54.

[7] The authors of FM 3–24 credit Max Manwaring, the author of the SWORD Model, or the Manwaring Paradigm, for this insight on legitimacy. The Manwaring Paradigm emphasizes the importance of legitimacy. The manual's analysis of legitimacy can be found in FM 3–24, paragraphs 1-113 through 1-120, on pages 37–39. One can find a summary of Manwaring's legitimacy-centered model in Edwin Corr and Stephen Sloan, eds., *Low-Intensity Conflict: Old Threats in a New World* (Boulder, CO: Westview Press, 1992), 12–16.

[8] FM 3–24, paragraph 1-116, on page 38.

[9] Ibid., paragraphs 5-7 through 5-49, on pages 154–173.

[10] For counterinsurgency (COIN) as the combination of various types of military operations (offense, defense, and stability operations), see the first illustration in FM 3–24, figure 1-1, 35.

[11] Mark Moyar, *A Question of Command: Counterinsurgency from the Civil War to Iraq* (New Haven: Yale University Press and Yale Library of Military History, 2009), 1–13. These pages briefly summarize various approaches to counterinsurgency. The short quotation is on page 3.

[12] The author thanks Jacqueline Hazelton of Harvard's Belfer Center for assistance in clarifying issues related to population-centric COIN and counterguerrilla-focused efforts.

[13] T.X. Hammes, in *The Sling and the Stone: On War in the 21st Century* (St. Paul, MN: Zenith Press, 2006), popularized the term *fourth generation warfare*, or evolved insurgency.

[14] The following article stresses the importance of multiple lines of operation, with Information Operations running throughout all of them: LTG David Barno, USA, "Fighting 'the Other War': Counterinsurgency Strategy in Afghanistan, 2003–2005," *Military Review* 87, no. 5 (September–October 2007), available at <http://usacac.army.mil/CAC2/MilitaryReview/Archives/English/MilitaryReview_20071031_art006.pdf> .

[15] David Kilcullen, *The Accidental Guerrilla: Fighting Small Wars in the Midst of a Big One* (New York: Oxford University Press, 2009), xiii–xix, 28–38.

[16] Private conversations between the author and intelligence analysts, 2009 and 2010. The late Special Envoy for Afghanistan and Pakistan, Ambassador Richard Holbrooke, also believed that charitable donations to the Taliban were more lucrative than drug-trafficking. This fact was a staple of his public presentations.

[17] On the dominance of narcotics-related issues in the war in Afghanistan, see Gretchen Peters, *Seeds of Terror: How Heroin is Bankrolling the Taliban and Al Qaeda* (New York: Thomas Dunne Books of St. Martin's Press, 2009), 14–20.

[18] FM 3–24, paragraphs 5-90 to 5-116, on page 188–197; and David Kilcullen, *Counterinsurgency* (New York: Oxford University Press, 2010), 51–83.

[19] Galula, 11–28.

[20] FM 3–24, paragraph 1-67, 22–23, discusses troop-to-population ratios.

Chapter 7

[1] On comparative development, see the UN Development Program's Human Development Index and report, available at <http://hdr.undp.org/en/statistics/>. This report includes economics, education, health, security, and many other factors. Afghanistan has consistently been in the bottom 10 countries in the world. Along with the Department of State *Background Notes*, and the CIA *World Factbook*, there are many statistics on aid to Afghanistan on USAID's Web site at <http://afghanistan.usaid.gov/en/index.aspx>.

[2] Ashraf Ghani and Clare Lockhart, *Fixing Failed States* (New York: Oxford University Press, 2008), 75.

³ For a new study on the evolution of NATO's commitment to Afghanistan, see Andrew Hoehn and Sarah Harting, *Risking NATO: Testing the Limits of the Alliance in Afghanistan* (Santa Monica, CA: RAND, 2010), 25–40.

⁴ The current Constitution of Afghanistan, Afghan Year 1982, can be found in English at <http://www.afghan-web.com/politics/current_constitution.html> and its 1964 predecessor at <http://www.afghan-web.com/history/const/const1964.html>.

⁵ Author's calculation using the U.S. Embassy chart and an estimate of 28 million Afghans. Note that U.S. assistance throughout this operation has been more than the equal of all other aid from all other sources. International funds do not include non-U.S. international security assistance expenditures unless they are reflected in national aid totals.

⁶ Dobbins et al., 146, 157–158.

⁷ USAID statistics are from <http://afghanistan.usaid.gov/en/index.aspx> and a presentation by General Petraeus at RUSI, October 15, 2010, available at <http://www.rusi.org/events/past/ref:E4CB843C349F2E>.

⁸ Kenneth Katzman, *Afghanistan: Post-Taliban Governance, Security, and U.S. Policy* (Washington, DC: Congressional Research Service, August 17, 2010), 88–90, available at <http://assets.opencrs.com/rpts/RL30588_20100817.pdf>.

⁹ Prior to 2004, the PRTs had a chain of command separate from troop units. That was ended by Lieutenant General Barno, in part to create more unity of command and in part to free up Civil Affairs assets.

¹⁰ Written comment of anonymous NATO Supreme Headquarters Allied Powers Europe (SHAPE) reviewer to the author, November 18, 2010.

¹¹ U.S. figures to 2009 come from Kenneth Katzman, *Afghanistan: Post-Taliban Governance, Security, and U.S.* Policy (Washington, DC: Congressional Research Service, September 17, 2010), table 21, 91. Foreign data are adapted from Brookings, *Afghanistan Index*, table 3.15, available at <http://www.fas.org/sgp/crs/row/RL30588.pdf>.

¹² Hoehn and Harting, 33.

¹³ USAID statistics at <http://afghanistan.usaid.gov/en/index.aspx>.

¹⁴ Galula, 6–7.

¹⁵ Data from U.S. Central Command, various briefings.

[16] For data on casualties and causes of death, see Brookings, *Afghanistan Index*, tables 1.21 and 1.22, available at <http://www.brookings.edu/~/media/Files/Programs/FP/afghanistan%20index/index.pdf>.

[17] SHAPE reviewer.

[18] Examples of night letters are in a USCENTCOM release, available at <http://centcom.dodlive.mil/2010/08/29/taliban-aims-to-hinder-development-by-threatening-civilian/>.

[19] Testimony of (former) Under Secretary of State James K. Glassman before the Senate Foreign Relations Committee, March 10, 2010, available at <http://mountainrunner.us/files/congress/testimony/SFRC_20100310-GlassmanTestimony100310p.pdf>.

[20] United Nations Assistance Mission in Afghanistan, *Annual Report on Protection of Civilians in Armed Conflict*, August 2010, available at <http://unama.unmissions.org/Portals/UNAMA/Publication/August102010_MID-YEAR%20REPORT%202010_Protection%20of%20Civilians%20in%20Armed%20Conflict.pdf>; and Brookings, *Afghanistan Index*, figure 1.29.

[21] A short history of ISAF can be found at <http://www.isaf.nato.int/history.html>.

[22] Greg Miller and Josh Partlow, "U.S., Afghanistan Plan to Screen Cash at Kabul Airport to Prevent Corruption," *The Washington Post*, August 20, 2010, available at <http://www.washingtonpost.com/wp-dyn/content/article/2010/08/20/AR2010082004049.html>.

[23] ISAF J1 statistics from NTM–A briefing at NDU; and Brookings, *Afghanistan Index*, table 1.27.

[24] Conversations with various active and retired senior officers from USCENTCOM and U.S. Forces–Afghanistan, 2008.

[25] See account in Ronald E. Neumann, *The Other War: Winning and Losing in Afghanistan* (Washington, DC: Potomac Books, 2009), 41–50.

[26] Sean Maloney, "Afghanistan: Not the War It Was," *Policy Options* (Canada), (November 2010), 44.

[27] Various ABC–BBC and Asia Foundation Polls, 2005–2009. For January 2010 ABC–BBC polls, see <http://abcnews.go.com/images/PollingUnit/1099a1Afghanistan-WhereThingsStand.pdf>; and for October 2009 Asia Foundation polls see <http://asiafoundation.org/resources/pdfs/Afghanistanin2009.pdf>.

Chapter 8

[1] Many senior officials in Afghanistan dislike the *surge* term for various reasons. It is used here because it is commonly used in the United States. One should exercise great caution in drawing analogies between the Afghan surge and the complicated events of the surge in Iraq.

[2] Conversations between the author and two senior NSC officials, as well as a scholar who later participated in the review, spring 2010. This is also discussed in detail in Bob Woodward, *Obama's Wars* (New York: Simon & Schuster, 2010), 40–44.

[3] Woodward, 88–90, 99–109.

[4] *White Paper of the Interagency Policy Group's Report on U.S. Policy toward Afghanistan and Pakistan*, March 27, 2009, available at <http://www.whitehouse.gov/assets/documents/Afghanistan-Pakistan_White_Paper.pdf>. The short quotation is on page 6.

[5] General Stanley A. McChrystal, USA, COMISAF's *Initial Assessment* (declassified and redacted), August 30, 2009, available at <http://media.washingtonpost.com/wp-srv/politics/documents/Assessment_Redacted_092109.pdf>.

[6] Michael E. O'Hanlon, "Staying Power: The U.S. Mission in Afghanistan, Beyond 2011," *Foreign Affairs* (September/October 2010), 70.

[7] The best record of Washington decisionmaking at this point is Woodward, *Obama's Wars*.

[8] Eric Schmitt, "U.S. Envoy's Cables Show Worries on Afghan Plans," *The New York Times*, January 25, 2010, available at <http://www.nytimes.com/2010/01/26/world/asia/26strategy.html?_r=1&ref=karl_w_eikenberry>.

[9] Greg Jaffe, Scott Wilson, and Karen de Young, "U.S. Envoy Resists Increase in Troops," *The Washington Post*, November, 12, 2009, available at <http://www.washingtonpost.com/wp-dyn/content/article/2009/11/11/AR2009111118432.html>.

[10] President Obama, "Remarks by the President in Address to the Nation on the Way Forward in Afghanistan and Pakistan," West Point, New York, December 1, 2009, available at <http://www.whitehouse.gov/the-press-office/remarks-president-address-nation-way-forward-afghanistan-and-pakistan>.

[11] Brookings, *Afghanistan Index*, figure 1.15.

[12] O'Hanlon, 71; latest strength figures are in the unpublished Headquarters, ISAF, *Public Affairs Message Guidance* (unclassified), November 18, 2010.

[13] Presentation by a U.S. Army general officer in a nonattribution setting, Washington, DC, February 2, 2011.

[14] West Point speech.

[15] A nonattribution presentation by a U.S. Army general officer at National Defense University, February 7, 2011.

[16] For a précis of NTM–A's accomplishments and problems, see NTM–A, *Year in Review: November 2009 to November 2010*, available at <http://www.ntm-a.com/documents/enduringledger/el-oneyear.pdf>.

[17] Multiple conversations with a senior USAID employee deployed in Regional Command–East for multiple tours, summer and fall 2010.

[18] The plan is available at <http://www.comw.org/qdr/fulltext/0908eikenberryandmcchrystal.pdf>.

[19] The late Ambassador Richard Holbrooke also confirmed increased pressure on the enemy in his remarks at *The Atlantic*'s and *National Journal*'s Washington Ideas Forum, held at the Newseum, Washington, DC, October 1, 2010. The author here draws on his own notes from the presentation. See also Dexter Filkins, "U.S. Uses Attacks to Nudge Taliban Toward a Deal," *The New York Times*, October 14, 2010, available at <http://www.nytimes.com/2010/10/15/world/asia/15afghan.html>.

[20] ISAF Joint Command–Afghanistan, "Afghan, Coalition Forces Tally Another Successful Month in Afghanistan," news release, IJC Public Affairs Office, October 1, 2010.

[21] ISAF, *Public Affairs Message Guidance*. For a pessimistic interpretation of late fall security developments in Afghanistan, see "Special Report: November 2010 in Afghanistan," NightWatch, January 30, 2011.

Chapter 9

[1] Much of this section draws on Collins, "Afghan Reconciliation" and "The Way Ahead in Afghanistan." The author admits to being a conservative and an optimist on Afghanistan. Many are more pessimistic and favor a rapid drawdown. Some of their works are cited below.

[2] For a recent estimate that puts Taliban strength at only 25,000, see Slobodan Lekic, "Taliban Strength Unaffected by Allied Surge," *The Washington Post*, January 6, 2011, available at <http://www.washingtonpost.com/wpdyn/content/article/2011/01/06/AR2011010602522.html>.

[3] Peter Bergen et al., *The Year of the Drone: An Analysis of U.S. Drone Strikes in Pakistan*, 2004–2010, available at <http://counterterrorism.newamerica.net/drones>.

[4] U.S. Institute of Peace (USIP), "Remarks with Afghan President Hamid Karzai," May 13, 2010, available at <http://www.state.gov/secretary/rm/2010/05/141825.htm>. On the Biden trip, see Ray Rivera, "Biden Assures Karzai of Aid from U.S. Beyond 2014," *The New York Times*, January 11, 2011, available at <http://www.nytimes.com/2011/01/12/world/asia/12afghan.html>.

[5] Operation *Enduring Freedom* casualty data can be found at <http://icasualties.org/oef/>.

[6] Author's notes of General Kayani's presentation at the New America Foundation, Washington, DC, March 25, 2010.

[7] From ISAF J1 statistics. See also, Brookings, *Afghanistan Index*, figure 1.27, 14, and the December 2010 update of the index at <http://www.brookings.edu/~/media/Files/Programs/FP/afghanistan%20index/index.pdf>.

[8] On U.S. polls, see *The New York Times*, October 15 and 16, 2010, summarized at <http://atwar.blogs.nytimes.com/2010/10/15/afghan-war-is-off-the-voters-radar/>.

[9] Jens Ringsmose and Christopher Schnaubelt, "Sharing the Burden in Afghanistan? An Appraisal of NATO's ISAF Mission," unpublished paper, September 2010, 1, 17–18, cited with the permission of Dr. Schnaubelt. See also Andrew Hoehn and Sarah Harting, *Risking NATO: Testing the Limits of the Alliance in Afghanistan* (Santa Monica, CA: RAND, 2010), 51, figure 4.

[10] This was the cost estimate in the President's final decision memorandum before the surge. See Woodward, 390.

[11] David S. Cohen, U.S. Department of Treasury, "Treasury Official on Terrorist Finance in Afghanistan, Pakistan," available at <http://www.america.gov/st/texttranseng-lish/2010/January/20100128150308eaifas0.2595026.html#ixzz0zhrc8EXS>.

[12] Alex Rodriguez and Laura King, "Reconciliation Efforts with Afghan Militants Face Major Obstacle," *Los Angeles Times*, June 29, 2010, available at <http://articles.latimes.com/2010/jun/29/world/la-fg-pakistan-haqqani-20100630/3>.

[13] Scott Shane, "Pakistan's Plan on Afghan Peace Leaves U.S. Wary," *The New York Times*, June, 27, 2010, available at <http://www.nytimes.com/2010/06/28/world/asia/28taliban.html>.

[14] Ruth Rene, ed., *Afghanistan in 2010: A Survey of the Afghan People* (San Francisco: Asia Foundation, 2010), 18, figure 2.2; 72, figure 7.1.

[15] Michael Hastings, "The Runaway General," *Rolling Stone*, June 22, 2010, available at <http://www.rollingstone.com/politics/news/17390/119236>.

[16] Detailed reports on the National Solidarity Plan can be found at <http://www.nspafghanistan.org/>.

[17] The communiqué of the Kabul International Conference on Afghanistan, July 2010, available at <http://unama.unmissions.org/Portals/UNAMA/Documents/Kabul%20Conference%20Communique.pdf>.

[18] For the basic COMISAF COIN Contracting Guidance, see <http://www.isaf.nato.int/images/stories/File/100908-NUI-COMISAF%20COIN%20GUIDANCE.pdf>.

[19] James Risen, "U.S. Identifies Vast Mineral Riches in Afghanistan," June 13, 2010, available at <http://www.nytimes.com/2010/06/14/world/asia/14minerals.html>. In Karzai's May 13, 2010 presentation at USIP, there was speculation by his party that the value of the minerals may be as much as $3 trillion. See transcript at <http://www.state.gov/secretary/rm/2010/05/141825.htm>. The U.S. Geological Survey estimates the total at $1 trillion. See Under Secretary Stephen Hormats, "Remarks at Afghanistan Minerals Roadshow," September 29, 2010, available at <http://www.state.gov/e/rls/rmk/2010/149240.htm>.

[20] For a thoughtful examination of Indian-Afghan relations, see C. Christine Fair, *India in Afghanistan and Beyond: Opportunities and Constraints* (New York: Century Foundation, 2010).

[21] Sandy Berger and Richard Armitage, chairs, *Independent Task Force Report: U.S. Strategy for Pakistan and Afghanistan* (New York: Council on Foreign Relations, November 2010), 21. The author of this monograph was a member of the task force but disagreed with some of its conclusions.

[22] Ibid., 38.

[23] See the official declaration by NATO's heads of state entitled Lisbon Summit Declaration, available at <http://www.nato.int/cps/en/natolive/official_texts_68828.htm?mode=pressrelease>. For Karzai's statement, see the transcript at USIP, "Remarks with Afghan President Hamid Karzai," May 13, 2010, available at <http://www.state.gov/secretary/rm/2010/05/141825.htm>.

[24] U.S. Army general officer, February 7, 2011.

[25] For a different view that argues for an immediate and rapid drawdown of U.S. troops, see Afghanistan Study Group, *A New Way Forward: Rethinking U.S. Strat-*

egy in Afghanistan (Washington, DC: Afghanistan Study Group, 2010), available at <http://www.afghanistanstudygroup.org/read-the-report/>. For a critique of this report, see Joseph Collins, "No Way Forward: Afghanistan Study Group Report Falls Short," *Armed Forces Journal*, November 2010, available at <http://www.armedforcesjournal.com/2010/11/4858188>.

[26] U.S. Army general officer, February 2, 2011.

[27] For Mullah Omar's guidance, see *Code of Conduct for the Mujahidin of the Islamic Emirate of Afghanistan*, August 2010, an unclassified document translated by the U.S. Government's Open Source Center, August 2010.

[28] Dexter Filkins, "The Taliban Don't Seem Ready to Talk," *The New York Times*, January 23, 2010, available at <http://www.nytimes.com/2010/01/24/weekinreview/24filkins.html?_r=1&scp=1&sq=dexter%20filkins%20king%20of%20saudi%20arabia&st=cse>.

[29] David Rohde, "7 Months, 10 Days in Captivity," *The New York Times*, October 18, 2009, available at <http://www.nytimes.com/2009/10/18/world/asia/18hostage.html?pagewanted=2&sq=david%20rohde%20october%202009&st=cse&scp=1>.

[30] Peter Bergen, "The Front: The Taliban-Al Qaeda Merger," *The New Republic*, October 19, 2009, available at <http://www.tnr.com/article/world/the-front>.

[31] Claudio Franco, "The Tehrik-E Taliban Pakistan," in *Decoding the New Taliban: Insights from the Afghan Field*, ed. Antonio Giustozzi (New York: Columbia University Press, 2009), 282. For a more authoritative statement by a leader of the Pakistani Taliban, see Chris Allbritton, "Pakistan Taliban Commander Vows to Expand Fight," Reuters, September 29, 2010, available at <http://www.alertnet.org/thenews/newsdesk/SGE68R0IU.htm>. For a full exposition of the complex al Qaeda–Taliban relationship, see Reidel, *The Search for Al Qaeda*, 61–84, 116–124.

[32] For details on the progress of the NATO Training Mission in Afghanistan in 2010, see their first year anniversary report, available at <http://www.ntm-a.com/documents/enduringledger/el-oneyear.pdf>.

Conclusion

[1] See interview with Major General Curtis M. "Mike" Scaparrotti, USA, commander of Regional Command–East (RC–East), June 3, 2010, available at <http://www.defense.gov/transcripts/transcript.aspx?transcriptid=4628>. General Scaparrotti and his civilian

deputy, Dawn Liberi, noted that there would be nearly 300 civilian experts in RC–East by the end of 2010. A recently returned commander of a brigade in that region spoke in spring 2010 to an NDU audience concerning the unity of effort on stability operations and reconstruction that takes place at every level of command. There is competent staffing on all lines of operation—security, stabilization, development, government, rule of law—down to the brigade level. The best figures on civilian strength appear in Brookings, *Afghanistan Index*, table 1.15, 9.

[2] A mea culpa: for 4 years in the first Bush administration, I worked hard to keep defense and military assets out of counternarcotics work. Our thought then was that combating the insurgency was much more important than eradication efforts. The truth is that counternarcotic operations are essential for good counterinsurgency and for lowering governmental corruption and improving governance. I still believe that there is little need for eradication work until the drug lords' infrastructure has been demolished.

[3] The irreplaceable text on this subject is Peters, *Seeds of Terror*.

[4] Robert B. Oakley and T.X. Hammes, *Prioritizing Strategic Interests in South Asia*, INSS Strategic Forum, no. 256 (Washington, DC: NDU Press, June 2010), 1.

[5] This paragraph is a slightly revised version of the author's letter to the editor on Afghanistan issues in *Joint Force Quarterly* 58 (3[d] Quarter, 2010).

About the Author

Dr. Joseph J. Collins is currently Professor of Strategy at the National War College in Washington, DC. From 2001 to 2004, he was Deputy Assistant Secretary of Defense for Stability Operations and very active in plans and policy for the war in Afghanistan, as well as in the initial planning for Operation *Iraqi Freedom*. A retired Army colonel, he is a veteran of over a decade's service in the Pentagon, and has taught at the United States Military Academy at West Point, Georgetown University, and Columbia University. Professor Collins's many publications include books on the study of Soviet policy toward Afghanistan, international relations theory, and U.S. military culture. He has spent the last few years teaching and writing on the war in Afghanistan. Professor Collins is also the author of *Choosing War: The Decision to Invade Iraq and Its Aftermath* (NDU Press, 2008). A life member of the Council on Foreign Relations, he holds a doctorate in Political Science from Columbia University.

Capture or Kill

The Pursuit of the 9/11 Masterminds and the Killing of Osama bin Laden

by Nick Fielding and Yosri Fouda

Khalid Shaikh Mohammed and Ramzi Binalshibh, two of bin Laden's key lieutenants: the masterminds behind the attacks of September 11. Based on the only interview these masterminds of terror ever gave to the media as well as extensive follow-up research, *Capture or Kill* may be the closest we will get to the full inside story of the plot. While Mohammed and Binalshibh were among the world's most wanted men and hiding in a safe house in Pakistan, they summoned star al-Jazeera TV reporter Yosri Fouda for a one-of-a-kind exclusive. Fouda knew he might well be walking into a trap, as *Wall Street Journal* reporter Daniel Pearl had done only months before.

He took the risk, and, for forty-eight hours, Fouda listened as Mohammed, head of al-Qaeda's military committee, and Binalshibh, the link between Mohammed Atta and the senior al-Qaeda leadership, proudly claimed responsibility for the attacks on New York and the Pentagon—the first time al-Qaeda took direct responsibility—and detailed for the first time exactly how the plot was conceived and executed.

The authors, uniquely positioned because of their prior unprecedented access and research, deliver a thrilling account of what has happened since. What has changed in the intervening years to this insidious global network? How does Osama bin Laden's capture and death affect its continuing operation? This is a must-read for anyone who wants to know not only the full truth behind September 11, but also the implications of recent events for the future of global security.

$14.95 Paperback

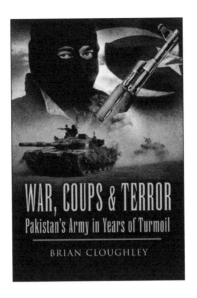

War, Coups, and Terror

Pakistan's Army in Years of Turmoil

by Brian Cloughley

In recent years, Pakistan has changed from being a state of regional strategic significance to one of major global importance. Its geographical position and delicate religious mix, coupled with a complex political structure and its status as a nuclear power, have ensured that its actions—and inactions—have attracted close scrutiny since 9/11 and the declaration of the "War on Terror." Yet there remains widespread disagreement among political and military analysts as to the real position of this enigmatic nation.

In *War, Coups, and Terror*, Brian Cloughley explores the underbelly of Pakistan's military and its controversial role within the Pakistani government since Zulfiqar Ali Bhutto came to power in 1971. An insider with links to Pakistan's past and present senior officers, Cloughley provides a unique insight into the Army's influence and position as a force in the fight against al-Qaeda and the Taliban, as well as an account of operations against the 2003–2004 tribal uprising. His coverage of military-political relations will fascinate those who seek a closer understanding of this enigmatic and complex country and its ambitions, affiliations, and loyalties.

$24.95 Hardcover

Reluctant Hero

A 9/11 Survivor Speaks Out About That Unthinkable Day, What He's Learned, How He's Struggled, and What No One Should Ever Forget

by Michael Benfante and Dave Hollander

On Tuesday, September 11, 2001, Michael Benfante went to work, just like he had day after day, at his office on the eighty-first floor in the World Trade Center North Tower. Moments after the first plane struck just twelve floors above him, Benfante organized his terrified employees, getting them out the office and moving down the stairwells. On his way down, he and another coworker encountered a woman in a wheelchair on the sixty-eighth floor. Benfante, the woman, and Benfante's coworker then embarked on a ninety-six-minute odyssey of escape— the two men carrying the woman down sixty-eight flights of stairs out of the North Tower and into an ambulance that rushed her to safety just minutes before the tower imploded.

A CBS video camera caught Benfante just as he got out the building, and almost immediately, the national media came calling. Benfante sat on the couch with Oprah Winfrey, where she hailed him as a hero. Almost one year to the day after 9/11, Benfante got married, and the woman in the wheelchair sat in the front row.

That's the storybook ending. But in the aftermath of 9/11, Benfante began a journey fraught with wrenching personal challenges of critical emotional and psychological depth in *Reluctant Hero*. Benfante shares the trappings of his public heroism, the loneliness of his private anguish, and the hope he finds for himself and for us. Because all of us—whether we were in the towers, in New York City, or someplace else—are 9/11 survivors.

$24.95 Hardcover

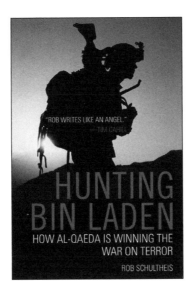

Hunting bin Laden

How al-Qaeda Is Winning the War on Terror

by Rob Schultheis

"I first met al-Qaeda before there was an al-Qaeda, way back in the winter of 1984. It was an encounter that came within a split second of costing me my life."

So begins Rob Schultheis's gripping account of his journey into the heart of one of the world's most dangerous places, on the trail of the world's most wanted man. A veteran war correspondent (he was one of a handful of Western journalists who covered the Russian war in Afghanistan from inside the country), Schultheis offers a firsthand look at how the seeds of al-Qaeda were planted by foreign jihadists in the 1980s, before most Americans knew what the word "jihad" meant. He then offers a radical assessment of why bin Laden remained at large, detailing the complicit role Pakistan has played in both offering him sanctuary and helping al-Qaeda establish an almost impregnable stronghold in the Middle East. Finally, fresh from a recent visit to Afghanistan and armed with analysis of current satellite imagery, Schultheis makes his case for where exactly Osama bin Laden was hiding—and why the U.S. government did not immediately act on this information.

$24.95 Hardcover

The Osama bin Laden Files
Letters and Documents Discovered by SEAL Team Six During Their Raid on bin Laden's Compound

On May 2, 2011, U.S. Navy SEALs and CIA operatives raided the secret compound of Osama bin Laden, killing the founder of the jihadist militant group al-Qaeda, which was responsible for the tragedies of September 11, 2001. A year after his death, documents and personal correspondence by bin Laden found in the compound have been made public for the first time, offering a rare glimpse into the mind of one of the most infamous terrorists in world history.

A treasure trove of documents, including correspondence between bin Laden and other al-Qaeda leaders, has been translated from Arabic, accompanied by analysis and background information from members of the Combating Terrorism Center at West Point. *The Osama bin Laden Files* details the decision making behind one of the most nefarious terrorist organizations of all time.

$12.95 Paperback